T0358049

With a passion for excellence and sharing her Airbnb secrets, **Juls Rollnik** is a Superhost, author, property developer, and a mum. This is her story of how, by a twist of fate, she fell into and then embraced the world of Airbnb. After her husband's brush with death and faced with the prospect of raising two children alone, without an income, Juls embarked on a mission to find financial independence. Along the way she discovered that her uncanny ability to make people feel special and her desire to create a fabulous experience for her guests combined to make Juls a 'kick ass' rockstar Airbnb Superhost. Juls takes you into the world of Airbnb hosting and shares the secrets she learned along the way to becoming the much loved host that she is.

'I wrote *Secrets of a Superhost* because I wanted to share my Airbnb secrets and help others become a Superhost, just like me.'

www.secretsofasuperhost.com

SECRETS OF A SUPERHOST

How to become an Airbnb rockstar

JULS ROLLNIK

BROADCAST

First published in Australia in 2022 by Sliding Doors (Aust) Pty Ltd

A catalogue record for this work is available from the National Library of Australia

ISBN: 978-0-6452373-7-5 Paperback
ISBN: 978-0-6452373-8-2 Ebook

Produced by Broadcast Books, www.broadcastbooks.com.au
Edited by Peter Vaughan-Reid and Bernadette Foley
Proofread by Puddingburn Publishing and Charle Malycon
Cover design by Liz Seymour, Seymour Design
Text design by Matthew Oswald, Like Design
Typeset in Bembo 13/18pt by Like Design
Front cover image by Ben Mack, Sydney, Australia
Author photo by Alec Rollnik
Printed by SOS Print + Media Group

This book would not have been written if it weren't for my husband's unwavering belief that I could do it. He never, ever gave up on me, and he pushed me so far out of my comfort zone, I could have committed mariticide on more than one occasion! This one is for you, Adam.

It is also dedicated to my fellow Airbnb hosts. You are all stars, and I am honoured to have been part of the constellation.

Don't think about it – do it.

Contents

Author's Note ix

Introduction 1

1	In the Beginning	5
2	Mayfair or The Strand?	11
3	Who Owns It?	18
4	Getting It Right	22
5	What's Your Style?	26
6	Show and Tell	32
7	Know Your Worth	38
8	The Body Corporate	48
9	Getting Down to Business	54
10	The Road to Superhost	61
11	Back to School Again	73
12	The Cleaner	76
13	You Can't Win 'Em All	82
14	Boundary Lines	89
15	The Little Things	97

16   Let's Talk   109

17   Hiccups   117

18   Handle with Care   122

19   The Comforts of Home   135

20   COVID-19 Comes Knocking   142

21   Time to Say Goodbye   146

Superhost Checklists   149

Checklist 1: Choosing your apartment to rent
  out on Airbnb   150

Checklist 2: Fitting out your apartment
  – furnishings and style   153

Checklist 3: Preparing to launch on the Airbnb website   154

Checklist 4: Running your Airbnb   156

Checklist 5: Profit and loss   158

Airbnb Requirements to be a Superhost   160

Apartment Manual   161

Acknowledgements   173

Author's Note

During my Airbnb journey I have had many guests stay in my apartment in Melbourne. Almost all of them have enjoyed the experience, and I have had the privilege of sharing their experiences with them.

All the reviews and associated guests' names in the book are true. So are the stories, however, in these I have changed the guests' names in order to protect their privacy and save any potential embarrassment. Any mention of books, courses and people in this book are for reference purposes. I am not affiliated with any person or company for the promotion of their products.

This book is based on my Airbnb journey with my one-bedroom apartment. If you rent out a room in your home or your holiday house, some sections of this book may not be directly relevant to your situation, although the general principles will hold true.

Fantastic place to stay in the heart of the city! Juls was very welcoming and made sure our stay was perfect. The apartment is just superb with a very comfy bed and great furnishings. You will love this place. 🖤 Amy

Hi Juls, Wow, how lucky are we as first time Airbnb users to meet with the most amazing superhost there can possibly be. From the get-go you did everything possible to make sure there were no hiccups for us. Great details for entrance into your Zen-like, light-filled beautiful apartment. Hard to believe, I know, but your apartment is even better than the photos – and they sold me as soon as I saw them. The location is just a hop skip and a jump from the centre of Melbourne, but you don't feel as if you are in the hustle and bustle. Great cafés, restaurants, and bars in such close proximity. Everything that the other reviewers have written I second. The most immaculate, stunningly decorated, homely apartment you could wish to stay in. One complaint, Juls, I didn't want to leave and close your door for the last time … but, never mind, I'm booking again for June! Thanks for being so very friendly and for letting me extend at such short notice. See you soon. Bev and Steve

Introduction

Whatever you can do or dream you can, begin it.
Boldness has genius, power and magic in it.

Goethe

The seed for this book was planted back in January 2017. I was holidaying with my family in what I call my 'happy place', Queensland. We were staying in an apartment right on the beach in Surfers Paradise. Adam, my husband, and I had a daily ritual of rising at 5 am (there is something truly magical about starting your day when most people are still in a deep slumber). We would kick off with an invigorating walk along the beach, share our plans and dreams for the future, then finish with a refreshing dip in the sea. We returned one morning from our walk and swim and sat on our balcony drinking coffee. I was moaning about the standard of the accommodation we had stayed at over the previous few years and was perplexed as to why others didn't run their Airbnbs like I did.

Adam said, 'Juls, you need to write a book! You're such an incredible host. You've been a Superhost from the beginning. Our apartment is now in the Airbnb Plus group. You have insights you need to share with the community.'

That stopped me in my tracks and got me thinking. Many

hosts seemed to be missing the point of hosting. Over the years, I'd had lots of people share their 'shitty' Airbnb experiences with me. As soon as I mentioned I was an Airbnb host, someone would tell me about one of their horror stays. I've also had my own poor experiences as an Airbnb guest. So, maybe, I thought, just maybe, it's time to share some of Juls' magic with others, so they can create a bit of what I created.

The apartment where we were staying at the time could certainly have done with some of my magic. The location was perfect – a boutique apartment building on the beachfront. But the apartment itself was tired, and only the bare essentials were provided (no coffee plunger in sight). And that was only the first disappointment.

One of the first things I do when I arrive is check for the wi-fi codes. In this apartment, they were nowhere to be found. After about twenty minutes of searching for the codes (and my family having a nervous breakdown because they were desperate for their fix of the internet), I contacted the manager.

'Oh, sorry,' she said. 'I'll give them to you in the morning. It's after hours now and I'm not in the office and haven't got the internet codes.'

What! Had I heard correctly? We will have to wait until tomorrow to get the codes? You can't be serious! Shouldn't the codes be written down somewhere in the apartment, like in a manual or stuck to the fridge?

I was stunned that something so super important and simple was not readily available. That I had to wait a day to get the codes was ridiculous. It didn't even resonate with the manager that this was an inconvenience. 'Upstairs for thinking, downstairs for dancing', as my dad used to say. This would never have happened on my watch. My number one rule as a host is 'Move heaven and earth to look after your guests', and I mean, move heaven and earth.

Adam had a point. Maybe I should write a book to help hosts become better hosts, to help them tap into what it takes to be an exceptional host. There certainly seemed to be a need for such a book, and 'Miss Airbnb Royalty' (yes, I have been called that a few times by guests) was just the girl for the job.

You would think that would have been enough of a catalyst to get me started, but it didn't quite work out that way. I left Queensland brimming with ideas. I would share my tips for giving guests a memorable experience ('experience' is a word my guests continually use), but, as these things go, it went to the back of my mind. It wasn't until much later – two and a half years later – when I was in Bali on a yoga and meditation retreat, that I made a half-hearted attempt to start the book and was reminded why it was important.

I had my laptop with me at breakfast, and I was attempting to put a few words on the page. It didn't take long for me to put that aside and strike up a conversation with the guy who was sitting at the next table. The conversation soon steered its way to 'What do you do?' I mentioned I was an Airbnb host and was writing a book about my experiences, though in reality I'd barely written anything at that point.

The guy, John, looked at me as if to say, 'Are you kidding me?' He told me that he and his partner, Jane, were holidaying in Bali and were renting out their home on Airbnb for the very first time. What are the chances of that happening? Me attempting to write a book on Airbnb and meeting a first-time Airbnb host. You can't make this up!

John was keen to know all about the book and he took the opportunity to ask me questions – lots of questions – about hosting. In true Juls fashion, I started to share an array of hosting gems.

'You have to write this book,' he said. 'From what you've shared with me, this book will be gold!'

John couldn't believe his luck in meeting me and getting all this fabulous advice about running an Airbnb. He told me he had absolutely no idea about half the things I explained and was really grateful for all the tips I gave him. He was so excited, he said I had to meet his partner, Jane.

Up until that point, I hadn't committed myself to writing the book. However, that serendipitous moment was a game changer for me. After that conversation, I knew I had to write this book and share the secrets of my success.

I did meet Jane, and meeting her made me feel like the Rolling Stones on tour. She was just as excited as John about my book and couldn't wait to read it. Both John and Jane said it would be such a welcome read for so many people. I was intrigued to know why they felt that way. They told me that instead of telling people how to host, like a lot of books on Airbnb, I would be sharing my own personal experiences, which were far more relatable for people. Through my own successes, I would be sharing what worked for me.

Wow! I was genuinely humbled. It wasn't just going to be another 'how to' book. I would be taking people on a journey where they could see, through my eyes, what being a host is all about. Meeting that gorgeous couple was the moment I knew 'why' I had to write this book. I will always be grateful to them.

1

In the Beginning

It's not the destination, it's the journey.

Ralph Waldo Emerson

Did I want to be an Airbnb host? Absolutely not! No way José was I going down the Airbnb path, I wasn't interested in the slightest.

There is an old saying, 'If you want to make God laugh, tell him about your plans.' While I had no intention of becoming an Airbnb host, God clearly had other ideas.

Back in 2013, my whole world fell apart – lock, stock and two smoking barrels. I remember the moment like it was yesterday. I was sitting in the backyard having a coffee and enjoying the warm rays of the sun when my husband Adam came outside and looked at me – a blank expression on his face.

'I need to talk to you,' he said. 'I've seen Bruce [our doctor]. He ran some tests and I have bowel cancer.'

Adam had the big 'C', and death was a realistic outcome.

This wasn't my first rodeo with cancer. I had been down this road a few times before. When I was seventeen, my beautiful mum, Irene, was diagnosed with breast cancer. She had a mastectomy, and the cancer went into remission, but it came back with a vengeance a few years later. This time it spread aggressively to her bones. Mum died six weeks after her second diagnosis. I was twenty-two years old.

In a cruel twist of fate, my oldest sister, Denise, was diagnosed with cancer a few weeks before Mum died. Denise's cancer progressed a lot slower than Mum's. It dragged on for a few years. Eventually she succumbed to it. That same year, my grandmother died of cancer. I was twenty-four.

Now Adam? Cancer? Those two words didn't go in the same sentence. Adam was such a fit and healthy forty-four year old man. He would start his day at 5 am with a ritual of a ridiculous number of sit-ups and push-ups, before jumping on his bike to ride to work and punch out a twelve-to-fourteen hour day. Throw in being an avid tennis player, jogger, and the most driven man I have ever met. I felt like I had been well and truly sucker-punched.

Adam's cancer was a ticking time bomb. If it could not be cured (and that was a real possibility), Adam would be dead and I would be left with two kids to support (Alec, twelve, and Paris, ten), a huge mortgage, and no savings. Up until that point, we had been living like a lot of people: pay cheque to pay cheque. Without Adam's income the kids and I would not be able to continue living the life we were used to. I had to do something to ensure our financial security. I had been a stay-at-home mum for a number of years, so I wasn't going to be setting the world on fire. What the hell was I going to do?

That question would have to wait, because we were suddenly plunged into a two-week whirlwind of blood tests, MRIs, CT scans, ultrasounds, and surgeon appointments (bowel and liver surgeons). After the tests, Adam's liver surgeon gave us the awful news that the bowel cancer had metastasised and spread to Adam's liver, and we were in for the fight of our lives.

Adam is one of the bravest, most courageous human beings I know. I had only ever seen him cry at his grandmother's (Oma's) funeral. But while we sat in our car trying to process the magnitude of the situation, he burst into tears.

'I'm not scared of dying,' he said. 'It's saying goodbye to you and the children and not being able to watch my children grow up that makes me so sad.'

And that was it; we were both uncontrollable messes in puddles of tears.

Adam was in the throes of stage IV liver cancer. To put it in perspective, there is no stage V. Eradicating the growing mass in Adam's body was a matter of utmost urgency.

Two weeks after Adam's initial diagnosis he was being prepped for surgery. This was the first of two operations Adam had to have. This operation was to remove the cancer from the bowel and a part of the cancer from the liver. We were told that the operation is a very long and intricate procedure, and that Adam would most likely have to have a stoma (an opening created in the abdomen to allow the faeces to leave the body) and colostomy bag. Adam is an incredibly private and proud man. The words 'stoma' and 'Adam' definitely did not go hand in hand. I think Adam was more traumatised by the thought of having a stoma inserted than the actual operation. I was just trying to hold my shit together (no pun intended).

After about seven and a half hours on the operating table, Adam emerged, still alive, still breathing and with no colostomy bag in sight. In that operation they removed a piece of his bowel and about ten per cent of his liver.

Four months later, he was back on the operating table. Although they took another sixty-five per cent of his liver this time around, this operation was shorter (about two to three hours) and less traumatic. Fortunately for Adam, he only had four 'spots' of cancer on his liver, and they were able to be surgically removed (and the liver happens to be the only major organ with the capacity to grow back to full size and functionality after an operation like this).

After this second operation, Adam started six months of fortnightly chemotherapy sessions, in an effort to destroy any stray cancer cells. It would be five years before the doctors would be able to say, with any certainty, that Adam was totally cancer free. In the meantime, while it was still hanging over our heads, I went back to thinking about what I could do to ensure our financial security if things took a turn for the worse.

My financial education begins

As luck would have it, I fell upon a book called *Rich Dad Poor Dad* by Robert Kiyosaki.[1] It had been sitting on my bookshelf for God knows how long, and I was going to 'get around to reading it' one of these days. Yeah sure! This day, however, it stared back at me. Coincidence? I don't know. I was searching for a way forward in a desperate situation, perhaps it would help.

Rich Dad Poor Dad was my introduction to financial education, and through it I learned of Robert Kiyosaki's wife, Kim Kiyosaki, the co-founder and CEO of The Rich Dad Company and an advocate of financial education, particularly

---

[1] *Rich Dad Poor Dad* is a 1997 book written by Robert Kiyosaki and Sharon Lechter. It advocates the importance of financial literacy, financial independence and building anana wealth through investing in assets, real estate investing, starting and owning businesses, as well as increasing one's financial intelligence.

for women. She wrote, 'Today, more than ever, we, as women, can no longer depend on someone else, be it our husband or partner, our parents, our boss, or our government to take care of us financially.[2]

I was intrigued and wanted to learn more about Kim Kiyosaki. Wasn't this exactly what I needed? I rushed out and bought myself a copy of her book, *Rich Woman*.[3] What a find! I devoured it in one sitting, and it was a game changer for me. Not only was it inspiring, but it gave me hope. I was absolutely pumped to learn all I could. So, with bucket loads of life experience and the survival of my family as motivation, I knew I just had to get on with it, and get on with it I did.

Reading Kim's book moved me in the direction of property investing. I had no idea where this path was going to lead, but I thought this would be a good place to begin.

I started by attending a two-hour seminar with Wakelin Property Advisory. It was a sensational seminar, and I learned lots of valuable information. This course led me to attend a two-day property investment course with Property Planning. Once again, it was a brilliant course, and it had some great speakers.

In both courses I loved hearing from the accountants, bankers and lawyers – learning about the intricacies of property investing and the team you need to have around you for success.

After these two seminars I was hooked.

A new opportunity: Airbnb

Around this time, in about 2014, Adam mentioned a colleague who had listed her investment property as accommodation on

---

[2] Kim Kiyosaki, *Rich Woman*, Rich Press, Scottsdale, US, 2006, p. 45

[3] *Rich Woman* is a book on investing for women.

Airbnb. The idea popped into his mind that we could buy an apartment and do the same. Airbnb as a short stay provider was not as common and accepted as it is today and so it felt as if it was going to be a step into the unknown.

Adam thought I would make a fantastic host because I am good with people, a great communicator, and he knew I would give it my all and then some. I did not know the first thing about Airbnb and I thought he was nuts. It took some serious persuading to get me on board, but eventually I saw the merit of this idea and threw my hands up in the air and said, 'Okay let's do this.'

Secret # 1: Life is unpredictable and opportunities sometimes arise unexpectedly

Even in your darkest hour, magic can happen. When all seems lost, opportunities can arise from unexpected places. Be open to possibilities, have faith in yourself, and seize the day! Just remember: 'When you are going through hell, keep going.' Winston Churchill

2

Mayfair or The Strand?

Buy land they're not making it anymore.

Mark Twain

You may already own the property you want to rent as an Airbnb, but I had to buy a property, and finding the right apartment took a lot of time, energy, and research.

Initially, I was pretty keen on buying an apartment in South Yarra. South Yarra is a gorgeous suburb in Greater Melbourne, Australia. It has an abundance of beautiful Art Deco apartments and lovely tree-lined streets. It is surrounded by hipster boutique shops, cool cafés and bustling restaurants. It is also close to many of the major sporting venues Melbourne boasts, such as the Melbourne Cricket Ground and the National Tennis Centre, and is only a hop, skip and a jump away from the city.

Another reason I was keen on buying in South Yarra was it was one of the highest capital growth areas in Melbourne. So, I went to loads of open houses and auctions to get a feel for the suburb. When I had done all the research I felt was necessary, I started to look for my dream apartment.

Buying an apartment in South Yarra proved easier said than done, as the ones that ticked my boxes seemed to tick everyone else's boxes too. Time and time again I got outbid at the auctions I attended. After what seemed like months of missing out on my dream investment, I realised I had to widen the net — I just wasn't in a financial position to buy a one-bedroom apartment in an Art Deco building in South Yarra. Those rare gems were too highly sought after and carried a premium price tag. My dream was fast becoming a nightmare. I had to consider some other options.

City centre location

The next possibility was the central business district (CBD). Property in Melbourne's CBD doesn't have the potential for capital growth that South Yarra has, but it certainly does well from a cashflow perspective. This is because visitors to Melbourne are very happy to stay in the city itself. One of the big upsides for me was the affordability of a CBD apartment. Back in 2015, Art Deco apartments in South Yarra could go as high as $750k+, whereas apartments of a similar ilk in the CBD were going

I needed to find an apartment that would be attractive to travellers.

for around $450k. This was more within my price range, so I decided to switch my focus from South Yarra to the CBD.

What was not negotiable was that I wanted an apartment in a boutique block. I wasn't interested in an apartment in a high-rise block, where there could be anywhere up to 150 apartments. I wanted an apartment in a small block — which is generally easier to manage because there are fewer people involved — and preferably in an Art Deco building with character and charm. I was already visualising what my apartment was going to be like and what was going to appeal to guests staying in my Airbnb.

When something is in limited supply it will grow in value over time. New high-rise apartments are being built all the time, and so there is no scarcity factor, but they do not make Art Deco buildings anymore. That era came to an end in the late 1930s. As well, Art Deco buildings are generally well constructed and reasonably spacious. For these reasons, well located Art Deco apartments often generate good capital growth.

However, I needed to find an apartment that would be attractive to travellers and others looking for Airbnb accommodation. After doing a lot of the grunt work on my own when I was looking in South Yarra, I felt I needed to find a real estate agent I could build a solid relationship with and who understood exactly what I was looking for. I wanted someone who knew the city well and who had an ear to the ground for quality properties. I got lucky at the first inspection I went to when I crossed paths with an agent named John Fuller. John was one of those gentlemen from a former era: distinguished, dapper and with impeccable manners. He had been a city agent for many years and nothing got past him. If it was on the market, John knew about it. If it was off market, John knew about it. We hit it off immediately. What really struck me about John was that he was a great listener. He listened to what I was looking for in an apartment, and he delivered. While other agents wanted to show me everything on their books, John was more discerning and didn't waste my time.

Village feel

John showed me a couple of apartments, and while they were lovely and ticked a lot of my boxes, none of them was 'the one'.

We were close, but no cigar just yet. However, my luck was about to change. John told me about a one-bedroom apartment in a lovely boutique building in a fabulous part of town. My interest was immediately piqued.

I arrived in Hardware Street, a quaint residential lane that oozed charm and character, and I was immediately taken with the 'village' feel of the place. There were few cars, gorgeous trees lined the footpath and the neighbourhood had lots of groovy cafés and cool bars. People were milling about creating a great vibe and energy, and a café across from the apartment building had a line of customers stretching halfway down the street – impressive!

I was immediately taken with the 'village' feel of the place.

Keyless entry

The building itself was nestled between two cafés. Some of the apartments had Juliet balconies, which complemented the character of the street perfectly. I also noticed the entry to the building was keyless. That was a big ticket item for me because it meant I wouldn't have to install a lockbox (to allow guests to get the key for the building and for the apartment) or meet and greet guests. To install a lockbox I would need to get approval from the body corporate, and they can be a nightmare – anything to avoid having to go down that path was a bonus. With keyless entry I would be able to send the code to my guests and they could check-in themselves, as I also planned to install a keypad on the front door of the apartment. This was looking more and more promising by the minute.

The apartment for sale was one of the apartments in the

building with a beguiling Juliet balcony that overlooked the picturesque Melbourne laneway. Across the way was a lovely brownstone building that encapsulated the village feel of the street. Although the building wasn't Art Deco, which is what I had been looking for, the apartment itself was something special – warehouse-style with vaulted concrete ceilings and metal beams that gave it an industrial New York loft feel. The high ceilings, polished floorboards and open plan design created a sense of voluminous space, and the abundant natural light from the large windows that overlooked the laneway took my breath away. A bonus was the double glazing – the apartment was so quiet you could hear a pin drop. It had a definite Zen feel about it.

See the vision

Being vacant, the apartment was bare, which a lot of potential buyers find far less appealing than a fully furnished apartment. The months I'd spent at 'opens for inspection' and auctions where I'd been outbid were not wasted, as those experiences had given me the ability to visualise what the apartment might look like. I could see the vision. This was 'the one'.

I put in an offer and it was accepted. I had my dream apartment in a fantastic location – one that ticked all the Airbnb boxes. It was time to get this baby up and running. Little did I know life was about to change on a grand scale!

Weighing up the options: Capital growth vs cash flow

It is worth noting that any property purchase will usually involve a compromise between capital growth and cash flow. By choosing an apartment in a funky part of downtown Melbourne, a honey pot for tourists, I was maximising our cashflow potential. I knew the apartment was in a highly sought-after location, and I anticipated, rightly, that our apartment would attract guests because of this. However, being a CBD apartment, I knew I would not get the same capital growth as I would in South Yarra. The main reason for this is because there are lots of apartments in the city (and they always seem to be building new ones), and because the CBD is not where most people want to live. This keeps a lid on capital growth in the CBD for most properties. Was it the right choice? That question is difficult to answer. However, as I explain in the following chapters, I consistently had very high occupancy rates — more than eighty per cent — and I was able to charge a premium price. So, I accomplished everything I set out to achieve.

If, like me, you choose a city location, you may well get very high occupancy rates but miss out on high capital growth. The important thing is to proceed with your eyes open and make the choice that is right for you.

Checklists

At the back of this book I have included a number of 'checklists'. These identify, in a summary way, all the things you will need to look for when you are considering where to locate your Airbnb. There are checklists for all the major things you need to know about buying, owning and running your Airbnb.

Secret # 2: Location will drive your bookings

Location is the drawcard of your Airbnb, so choose wisely when buying, and highlight your location in your listing. Crowd pullers, like sports and entertainment venues, restaurants and bars, a beautiful beach, or a picturesque village, are important, but so too is the convenience of transport, supermarkets, and cafés.

3

Who Owns It?

The first thing we do, let's kill all the lawyers.
William Shakespeare, *Henry VI*, Part 2

Before I set up my Airbnb business, I had to give some thought to who was going to own and run the business – the legal structure. I could own it outright by myself, I could own and run it in partnership with Adam (or someone else), or I could set up a company. It was an important question, and one you should ask yourself right at the beginning. It is much better to do it at the start because changing the corporate structure (who owns the property) later can be costly. You may have to pay stamp duty, for example, and so better to get it right from the outset.

After attending various property investment courses and with a barrister for a husband, I decided that the best approach for me was to establish a company to own the apartment and to operate the business. When the apartment purchase went through, the company became the owner. Even though I was the host, I acted on behalf of the owner of the property, which was the company.

There were a number of reasons for this approach, including

the fact that if there was ever a problem and a guest sued, they would have to sue the company as the property owner, not me. For example, if a guest slipped over on the bathroom floor and broke their wrist, they would have to sue the company which, except for the mortgaged apartment, did not own any assets or have much cash in the bank. So while an injured guest *could* sue the company, they're less likely to do so, because even if successful, they would not get much, if any, money.

You might think such a scenario is unlikely, and you would be right. In the five years I had my apartment rented out on Airbnb, I didn't have any major incidents, accidents, or unfortunate events. No-one threatened to sue me, no-one slipped on the floor and injured themselves, no-one fell down the fire-escape stairs, and I didn't have any major damage occur at my apartment. In fact the worst thing that happened was that a guest spilt some red wine on a pillow – hardly a Shakespearian tragedy.

If something unfortunate and serious had happened, however, the consequences could have been significant. Personal injuries can result in significant payouts, so insurance companies will look for any legitimate reason to deny a claim. For example, if a guest slips and falls over after your cleaner forgets to properly dry the floors after mopping, then they may look to deny liability. The guest sues for negligence and the insurance company says it's not paying because the cleaner (your agent) did not ensure the floor was dry and safe to walk on. You, as the apartment owner and Airbnb business operator, could face significant exposure running into hundreds of thousands of dollars (or even millions of dollars – depending on the injury).

The chances of something like that happening are low,

but because the consequences can be so severe, I knew it was important to have the proper structures in place to protect my assets. Having the company owning the property and employing me to run the business provided me with a level of asset protection. With the company as the legal entity that owned the apartment and operated it as an Airbnb, it was quite unlikely the guests could, in those types of scenarios, sue me personally, which would force me to sell the house I owned and lived in. As much as I liked my guests, I needed to protect the assets I owned in my personal capacity.

In my experience, insurance companies are always happy to accept your premium payments, but they are rarely so keen to pay out when it comes to you making a claim. They will often look to avoid or sidestep what, at first sight, might look to you to be an obvious liability. Insurance is important; you should get it. But just because you have insurance, don't think it will always protect you. You can't rely on insurance to save the day. It may do so, but it may not. If it does not do so, then you don't want to suffer financially.

An injured guest might decide to sue Airbnb as well, but even so you need to protect yourself as best you can. Having a company own the property and operate the business can assist with this.

In addition, if I was the legal entity owning and running the business, then the profits from running the business would be added directly to my personal income and would be taxed on that basis. Having a company own the business offers flexibility when it comes to dealing with profits (or losses). The company still pays tax, but there is more flexibility with that tax liability.

Financial and legal advice

What's right for me might not be right for you. You should obtain your own financial and legal advice from professionals you know and trust, before deciding what the best business set-up is for your circumstances. I strongly recommend you give the issue some thought right from the outset, and that you consciously decide what is the best business structure for you.

Setting up a company from scratch is actually fairly straight forward (you can do it online via the ASIC website). It might cost about $500 to do so but in the long term, that investment might save you from losing your house. Just be aware that, as with personal tax, you will have to submit end-of-year financial statements and a tax declaration for your company. If you prefer, you can engage an accountant to assist with these.

In summary, do not simply buy a property and start the business in your own name without considering the consequences. It is much easier and more sensible to set things up properly from the beginning rather than try to change things some time down the track.

> **Secret # 3: Get the legal structure right, from the get-go**
>
> Take some time to work out the best structure for owning your property and operating your business. Running an Airbnb is a business operation, so get some professional advice and work out the best structure for you.

4

Getting It Right

Before anything else, preparation is the key to success.
Alexander Graham Bell

It was now time to prepare the apartment to be run as an Airbnb. There was no way I could just list my apartment on Airbnb and open the doors. I didn't even have furniture! More importantly, I didn't know the first thing about Airbnb. There was obviously going to be some trial and error because this was all new to me; but I wanted, as much as possible, to get it 'right' from the outset.

Guest reviews are the currency of Airbnb

Reviews are key in getting people through the door. The reviews you get from your guests are your currency and your legitimacy as you build your business. I could not afford to kick things off with my trainer wheels on and hope for the best. One or two poor reviews, especially at the start, and I would be swimming against the tide. Better to follow that old chestnut, 'Slow and steady wins the race', than to charge off without proper preparation.

I am a huge believer in playing to your strengths, which for me are personality, communication skills, and an ability to make people feel 'absolutely fabulous, darling'. Organisation is definitely not on the list. (You do not want to see my filing system and my email inbox.) Neither are accounting and bookwork (more on those exciting subjects later). I am also highly strung, and I can get a little anxious; without direction and structure I sink like the *Titanic* very quickly. I really needed a plan.

Okay, Juls, I thought, I need to do an Airbnb course.

Airbnb course or tutorial to get up to speed

The property investment seminars had taught me a lot. Now I had to imbue myself with knowledge again. This would give me the information and confidence I needed to run a successful Airbnb business. The results were going to be far better if I had the right preparation, and a course would give me an overall picture about Airbnb and how to get this baby up and running.

When Adam was having chemo just after his cancer operations, I lived with a constant sense that something bad was about to happen. The intensity was off the charts. I was like a volcano waiting to erupt, my emotions bubbling and rising to the surface, never knowing when I was going to explode. I was on a very scary emotional roller coaster ride and couldn't have contemplated undertaking a course at that time. But Adam's chemotherapy was behind him now, and he had been to several of his six-monthly follow-up appointments. For the moment, the CT scans and MRIs

I could not afford to kick things off with my trainer wheels on.

were clear, and I was feeling calm again and ready to 'go back to school'.

I searched the internet for anything Airbnb – 'How to Airbnb', 'Setting up your Airbnb', 'Airbnb For Dummies' – and I came across two courses that interested me. The first was 'Airbnb Hosting Mastery: Run a business using your own home'. This was Airbnb 101 and right up my alley – a complete step-by-step guide that went from beginning the Airbnb process right through to launching the Airbnb. The video tutorials were great because they only went for about twelve to fifteen minutes. This was incredibly appealing to me as I have a very short attention span. I could also skip over topics I didn't think were relevant to me. It was a fantastic course and perfect for a novice like me.

The course taught me everything I needed to know about how to get my Airbnb ready for launch, so I decided to leave the second course until later.

Learning as much as you can before you start will make all the difference in helping you get off on the right footing, rather than trying to muddle your way through. As mentioned, reviews can make or break your Airbnb, and the more knowledge you have before you start, the more likely you are to get five-star reviews from the get-go, and the more likely it will be that you will become a successful host.

Airbnb website: a valuable resource

The other important preparatory work you should do is to build your Airbnb webpage, on the Airbnb website. The Airbnb website (when you set up an account and log in as a host) is a fantastic and powerful resource. Get to know the Airbnb website inside out and also look at what other hosts have done and what they have to offer. Looking at, and learning from, other successful Airbnb operators is a great way to improve your knowledge and will help you to build a successful Airbnb business.

Secret # 4: Prepare for your Airbnb success

You want your Airbnb to open with a bang not a whimper. Great reviews at the start will accelerate your success. Bad reviews, on the other hand, may mean you never get off the ground. Prepare your property to wow your guests, prepare your listing to stand out from the crowd, prepare your processes – cleaning, accounting, and communicating with guests – but first prepare *you* by ensuring you have the knowledge that you need.

5

What's Your Style?

Every design choice we make has a sensual effect on us.

Lebo Grand

The next step in the process was to fit out my apartment. I had absolutely no interior design skills, or so I thought. Adam and I had moved from place to place across the globe and were too busy with work and kids to think about interior decorating. I hadn't yet tapped into the art of home design. That was something I thought I would get around to when I eventually bought my dream home.

If you are a dab hand at decorating, you may want to skip this chapter. But if you are anything like me, and don't know the first thing about decorating and have no idea where to begin, then keep reading.

Interior designing: how hard can it be?

As I had no experience with interior design, I thought I'd get an interior designer to help me. Easy right? Wrong. Do you know how many interior designers are out there?

I asked friends for referrals. I asked friends of friends for referrals. I went online and researched interior designers. I was becoming more and more confused and overwhelmed. After what felt like a lifetime, I had a short list of three designers. I met with each one and quickly came to understand that this could cost me north of $20,000. Yes, you heard right. Just to put some furniture into a one-bedroom apartment could cost twenty grand. Not only could I not justify spending that kind of money, but also I didn't have a spare $20,000 lying around.

I decided to go to the shops and give it a crack myself. One step at a time, I thought. I had always liked the store Adairs, which sells home furnishings and home decoration products in stores all around Australia. I found their furniture fresh and affordable, and I thought the style would complement the apartment nicely. Much to my surprise, I discovered that Adairs offered a home decorating service. For a $100 fee, a designer would come to the apartment to discuss design options, I would go on site visits to look at furniture, accessories and art selections, and I would receive personal hand-holding along the way. All this for $100. This was a far cry from the thousands and thousands of dollars I was quoted from interior designers to do the same thing. I felt like I had struck gold! I booked a consultation without a second thought.

I liked the designer, Denise, the minute I met her. She was larger than life and had an infectious personality. She was also an action-oriented person – a doer. She was exactly what I needed as I am more in my head and can take ages to make a decision. I felt we were going to be a great fit.

Denise took me through what Adairs could offer. She could tell I was nervous and had never done anything like this before. She was able to reassure me that I was in safe hands, and we were going to make the apartment absolutely spectacular.

She asked me lots of questions about the apartment and what I wanted from her and from the Adairs' service. Was I personally going to be using the apartment? Was it for a long-term rental or for short-term accommodation? She was able to listen to my vision for the apartment and was confident she would be able to help me bring the apartment to life. I liked that Denise wasn't pushy, as my foray into furnishing the space was making me feel vulnerable. She would offer suggestions on what she felt would be a great couch or side table or painting, but she was also keen for me to have input and form my own opinions. As we went along, I started to learn more about how interior styling worked. My own interior decorating instincts started to peek through, and I began to form my own opinions about what I thought would complement the apartment. Denise was very open to my ideas, and she encouraged me to trust myself. She was respectful and she listened to me.

The next step was to meet Denise at Adairs and at other outlets, so she could show me various furniture and accessory options. It was a huge job as we had a blank canvas to work with.

Interior design is important so take your time

Designing and setting up the interior of your Airbnb is important. It is important because that's mostly what your guests will see in the photographs on the Airbnb website when they are pondering whether to book your place, and because it will affect the experience your guests will have when they stay. So, my advice is to take your time with the process.

It is also important to have input into the decision-making process because you will differ in some of your choices with those of your stylist. If a piece of furniture doesn't feel right, then it probably isn't right for your space. Don't be afraid to speak up. I am big believer in always trusting your inner voice, that little word called 'intuition'.

Once we had chosen all the pieces (lounge suite, art, dining table, coffee table, lamps etc), Denise organised for everything to be delivered. As the apartment was taking form, my vision began to take shape too. This was a very exciting stage. I could see guests relaxing on the couch with a glass of wine. I could feel the joy the apartment was giving them. I was visualising my Airbnb in full flight. It's such a satisfying feeling when you can see it all coming together. My confidence was growing, and I started to believe in myself in a way I had never done before.

A space that isn't cluttered gives a sense of peace and calm.

One excellent piece of advice came from my sister who lives abroad and has a place where people can stay when they visit. She said, 'Juls, the best thing you can do is have your apartment like a hotel or serviced apartment. Make sure it is free of stuff.'

When you stay in a hotel or a serviced apartment, there is never any clutter. There can be statement pieces but there isn't 'stuff' everywhere. You want your Airbnb to be warm, comfy and clutter free. A space that isn't cluttered gives a sense of peace and calm. You don't want your guests to walk in and feel stressed or overwhelmed. You want the complete opposite.

It is also great for the cleaner, as they have to move everything when they dust. Can you imagine what it would be like for them if you have photos and knick-knacks all over the place? Not only would it take up a lot of their time, but also things could easily be knocked over and damaged. Your cleaner will be forever grateful if you keep your Airbnb free of ornamental bits and pieces, and so will your wallet.

I had some statement pieces in my apartment – including a few lovely prints – but I didn't have photos or knick-knacks.

A statement piece

A statement piece in your Airbnb can be a real showstopper, and I was very lucky to find a piece like that for my apartment. I was driving home one day, not long after setting up my Airbnb, when I noticed some unique pieces of furniture in the window of a homeware store that had just opened up. I was so intrigued, I pulled over to investigate.

The store had lots of exquisite pieces on sale. There was a vast amount of industrial furniture, which I absolutely love – coffee tables with wheels, gorgeous lamps and chairs – and I felt like I was in a New York loft. There were also some signs hanging on the wall that had street names with the longitude and latitude of the street written underneath. I thought a sign with 'Hardware Street' plus the longitude and latitude, would look awesome on the wall in my apartment. I spoke to the owner and he said that he could design one. It would be my very special statement piece. People would love it – it would look spectacular, be beautifully crafted and would anchor the apartment to its location.

It was lucky I stopped when I did and found my statement piece, as the shop didn't survive in that location for very long. You will know when you see your statement piece. It could be something you find on your travels abroad that has great meaning to you. It could be something you find in a vintage store. Or you could, like me, stumble across a rare shop with unique pieces. It doesn't matter where you find it, just make it unique to you or your Airbnb.

Secret # 5: Spend time on interior design and keep your Airbnb clean and clutter free

You want your Airbnb to look spacious and spotless, so keep it free of knick-knacks and bric-a-brac. Not only is a clutter-free space easy to clean, but your guests will also appreciate having places to put their own things and will adore the spacious, airy appearance of your property.

6

Show and Tell

Make it simple. Make it memorable. Make it inviting to look at. Make it fun to read.

Leo Burnett

Now that my apartment was styled, it was time to take some photos to upload onto the Airbnb website. I knew it was essential that my listing on the website had good quality photos that captured the essence of the apartment. Along with reviews, photos determine whether potential guests will want to stay at your Airbnb or not. Sometimes prospective guests will make their decision – or come up with a shortlist – based solely on photographs.

The better your photos, the more appealing your Airbnb is going to be to potential guests.

The better your photos, the more appealing your Airbnb is going to be to potential guests. Photos will either sell your listing, or they will turn people off in a flash. If they are dark, blurry, or grainy, then chances are, your prospective guest has already moved on to the next listing – even if your property is stunning in real life.

Professional photography

If you are a professional photographer or a skilled amateur, then you are all set. If not, I would highly recommend hiring a professional. You would not usually sell your house by taking photos on your iPhone; the same applies to your Airbnb. So, unless you are confident that your photos will do the trick, get a professional or phone a friend.

I knew I wasn't up to the task of taking the photos, so I opted to do both – get a professional photographer and phone a friend (or in my case my sister-in-law, Jessica, who is a dab hand with a camera). For the professional, I used the (then) free photography service provided by Airbnb. It took some time and some effort but ultimately, the result was well worth it.

What was vital to getting sensational and appealing photos, was making sure the photographer had a clear understanding of my brief. It was imperative that I connected emotionally with the photos. I wanted to feel something. I didn't want to just look at a photo and say that accommodation 'looks nice'. I wanted to be stirred. I wanted to be moved.

Because I had two photographers, the process of choosing which photos to use was overwhelming. I ended up making three piles of photos – a 'definite', a 'maybe' and a 'no' pile. If a photo really jumped out at me, it would go into the 'definite' pile. If I felt something but wasn't sure, then it would go into the 'maybe' pile. If I didn't really feel anything when I looked at a photo, the choice was easy – it went into the 'no' pile. I then narrowed the other two piles down and came up with my 'definites'.

I was happy with the work of the Airbnb photographer, but I am so glad I also asked Jessica for help; her photos were magical. When I saw them, I was blown away and found myself wanting to stay at my own Airbnb. There was an emotional element to them that captured the essence of my apartment and made it look and feel warm and homely.

Jessica had not only taken great photos of the apartment itself, she had also taken photos of the streetscape, the surrounding buildings, the foot traffic and the popular cafés in our thriving village. She took shots of the awesome café next door that sold the most inventive hot chocolate and whose food was really colourful, and the café across the way that often had a long line of people out front. She even captured a photo of an old classic car. It was gold! These photos were integral to showing the magic of Hardware Street. They were tantalising and helped to entice potential guests. Jessica had nailed the brief. Looking at the photos, my apartment was clearly the place to stay.

Do not underestimate the power of great photos. You want to connect people to your Airbnb, and good quality photos will do that.

Now for the blurb

Although a photo is worth a thousand words, I still had to write a blurb to go with the images I'd chosen for the listing. I knew writing the Airbnb blurb was going to really test me, because writing adverts, reviews, newsletters, even something as simple as a card, takes me absolutely forever. Whenever someone asks me to write them a recommendation or a review, I have a panic attack. I recently wrote a two paragraph review for someone, and it took me three days of writing and rewriting until I was happy with it. What a tripper!

For a while I had an astrology practice, and I used to write a monthly astrology newsletter. I kid you not, they would take me two weeks to write. I would do draft after draft until they were, in my eyes, perfect. By that time, I would pretty much be curled up in a foetal position from mental exhaustion. I don't recommend it as a very productive way to work. I would no sooner finish one newsletter, than I'd have to start the whole process again. The newsletters were very popular, but I ended up burning myself out and stopped writing the newsletters because I couldn't sustain producing them. So, imagine how I felt having to write an Airbnb advertisement. It was absolutely terrifying!

Lucky for me, Adam is the antithesis of a procrastinator. He kept pushing me to a deadline to 'go live' on Airbnb and helped me get on with it and get the job done. In the end, he had to push the 'post' button on the advert because I couldn't do it – I didn't think it was ready. If it was left up to me, I would have been sitting there for another week perfecting the copy.

Words are powerful and coming up with the right advertisement will make all the difference when it comes to a successful sale. A few years ago, when we were selling our home, our agent sent out the 'advertising person' from the office to write the advertisement for the listing. This person had been with the company for many years so I assumed she would be good. Boy, was I wrong! The advert she wrote was dull, boring, and uninspiring. I was unimpressed and conveyed this to my agent. He suggested I write it myself, and I said, 'What am I paying you for?' I asked him to send me someone who had imagination and vision. I wanted someone who could bring my home to life with their words.

Unsurprisingly, the agent wanted to keep my business and so he sent someone else. This new person was the antithesis of the first writer. She took in my surroundings and was interested in hearing about my history with our home. She listened to my stories, the memories we had as a family and what our home had meant to us. She was then able to convey all of that in the advertisement, which was nothing short of spectacular. It was emotional, captivating and hit that sweet spot. Mission accomplished.

When it comes to writing your advertisement, there is no need to reinvent the wheel.

A good way to come up with your advertisement for the Airbnb website is to look at how other Airbnb hosts have written their ads. You can learn a lot from what others have done. Pick your top three to five advertisements and use those as your starting point. You will need to change the words to suit your particular property – develop your unique spiel – but when it comes to writing your advertisement, there is no need to reinvent the wheel.

I knew my Airbnb advertisement had to be as alluring and captivating as possible. I wanted potential guests to feel they just *had* to stay at my apartment. The way I did that was to home in on the strengths of my Airbnb and its surrounds:

The charm and abundance of appeal of a bygone era! Combined with flair and verve, this perfect city hideaway provides convenient access to all of what Melbourne CBD offers.

Escape the bustle of the city in this Zen, stylish apartment just minutes from Melbourne Central Station.

Elegant, soothing details such as circular design motifs and clean lines make the space a tranquil, cosy sanctuary in the centre of the city.

Photos show the story, your blurb tells the story. Highlight your Airbnb's features and location, and make it stand out from the crowd.

Secret # 6: Engage a skilled photographer

Engage a professional (or skilful amateur) photographer to capture the heart and soul of your Airbnb. The better the photos, the more appealing your Airbnb will be.

7

Know Your Worth

When you are excellent you become unforgettable.

Oprah

I had my apartment, furniture, photos, and website blurb and now I was now ready to launch my Airbnb. But how much to charge? The last thing I wanted was to have a fabulous Airbnb but not get the financial rewards I deserved. I decided that I needed to be like Apple. Apple is a premium business. They charge a high price for their products and people buy them. Apple management and teams know their worth. Did I?

Knowing your worth is important because it has a big impact on how you run your Airbnb. These days I believe in myself and know what I am worth. But that wasn't always the case. I had great difficulty with this concept when I first started to see clients as an astrologer. I felt uncomfortable charging a lot of money for an astrology reading. Because I was starting out, I would charge a small fee and then feel obliged to give the clients a three-hour reading! As I built my practice, I still struggled with my worth. On the one hand, I knew I was a pretty fabulous astrologer who was providing a brilliant service to my clients, but on the other hand I had a 'slave' mentality and felt I had to give everything to the client. I felt guilty about charging more even though, clearly, I was undercharging at the time. I started to run myself into the ground, I resented what I was doing and I wanted to stop giving readings. I wasn't valuing my gift or my worth.

Some of the best advice I was given about knowing your worth was given to me by my fabulous sister Lyn, who told me this:

> *Juls, think about how much people are willing to pay for a haircut and colour. Some people easily spend $350 every month for a service like that. You are providing invaluable advice that can help improve people's lives, and you may see them only once in their lifetime. You can't put a price on that, can you?*

Lyn had a point! What did I do? I upped my price, and just like that I started to get busier and busier. It was a game changer.

I knew I would be able to charge top dollar for my apartment; it was a gem and I was putting the time and effort into making sure that my guests would really enjoy their stay. The apartment was in a very popular location in the beating heart of Melbourne. It was in a boutique apartment building, with stylish furniture, and it looked like a loft in Soho. Blood, sweat and tears had gone into making it a beautiful, comfortable abode.

Market position: what's your rate?

How much to charge is an important question because your pricing position in the market will affect your bookings and the type of people who come and stay. Put the price too low and you'll get lots of bookings, but you will also get people who may not treat your Airbnb the way it deserves. (Think, young party goers looking for a bargain and a place to party all night long. I was young once and loved to party, and I am happy for young people to party hard – just not at my place.) Put your price too high and you may not get many bookings and you'll miss out on the critical mass of reviews needed to drive further bookings.

> I had to get bums in beds to build momentum and get reviews.

I knew I had a winner on my hands, but initially I had to charge at a lower rate. I had to get bums in beds to build momentum and get reviews. I had not been tried and tested. I had no reviews, so why would someone pay top dollar for a place where no-one had stayed, despite it being a gem.

I listed the apartment at the lower end of the pricing spectrum – a price I thought would be attractive and affordable. I knew that once I got the guests through the door they would love it, and I had no doubt the five-star ratings would flow. I could increase my price later, once I had traction and good reviews. Believe me, reviews are one of the fundamental keys to your success as an Airbnb host. They will make or break you. Once the apartment had movement, and I had glowing reviews, I would put my price up. That was the plan.

Put in the effort and you'll get the rewards

As explained in the earlier chapters, I had put in quite the effort to ensure, as far as possible, that my apartment would be a success. My apartment was well located, overlooking a funky laneway in the CBD. I had, with the help of an interior stylist, fitted out the apartment with stylish furniture. I had fast wi-fi, a monster TV on the wall, Netflix, a coffee machine, new magazines on the coffee table, keyless entry, and an extremely comfortable bed. I was ready for launch but I was also as nervous as hell. Finally, it was time to pull the trigger.

I listed the apartment, and she went off like an absolute firecracker. People were booking it left, right and centre. I had my first booking request within fifteen minutes. I was so excited – and in shock – that it was booked so quickly. I knew that listing the apartment at such a low price was going to be very attractive to people, and it was.

This was my very first review:

Juls is a fantastic host, making me feel like a long-lost friend. Her apartment is an amazing warehouse conversion which drips style, yet nothing is overdone. One of my most memorable stays. The kitchen is well equipped, the sofas comfy and the balcony is perfect for enjoying a gaze down on to the bustle below. I wouldn't change a thing! I look forward to returning again soon! Oliver

The photos were gorgeous, the advertisement was enticing, and once guests stayed in the apartment they were blown away.

Steve and his partner, who lived in England, saw the listing and liked the look of the apartment. They had never been to Melbourne before, so when I confirmed their booking, I sent them some information about Melbourne and got this reply:

Hi Juls,

Thanks for confirming so quickly. We're really looking forward to our visit! Thanks very much for going to such an effort – that info will be a great help!

After their stay, Steve left this lovely review:

Melbourne is a fantastic place: friendly and welcoming. And so is this apartment. The location, description and photographs are all bang on. But I suspect that the reason that the property receives so many rave reviews is because Juls is such a fantastic hostess … Better than a hotel by far – highly recommended!

Jessica had captured the apartment and the village atmosphere perfectly, and her photos were working a treat. The fabulous reviews kept coming:

We had an absolutely delightful stay at Juls' urban nest! The apartment was picture perfect, with beautiful furnishing and decor, and had superb facilities, gadgets and amenities. The location is right on the doorstep of some of Melbourne's best bars, restaurants and shopping destinations but still manages to be a peaceful retreat within the beautiful and bustling city of Melbourne! Juls was such a gracious, friendly, helpful and kind host – we were honestly so lucky to have come across not only a fantastic place to stay but someone who made our experience above and beyond perfect. Juls has created such a calm and happy oasis in her Melbourne apartment, and we truly wish we had stayed longer! Would definitely recommend and hope to be back at some stage in the future. Jill

Thank you so much Juls for welcoming us into your home! You made the whole experience so easy and went above and beyond to ensure that we enjoyed our stay! The apartment was modern, clean, comfortable and beautifully decorated! You have really thought of everything! It was in such a great location, and your recommendations for local cafes are spot on! We couldn't recommend staying with Juls more highly after we had such a wonderful time there! Amazing apartment and host! Thanks so much! We can't wait to stay with you again soon! Jessica

From the moment we stepped into the apartment it immediately felt like home. Juls was very accommodating from the time I booked the apartment. The apartment is as beautiful as the pictures show and you can tell that Juls has put in a lot of effort to make the apartment feel cosy, it's so well furnished and has everything you will need for your stay. The location can't be beaten. I can't think of staying anywhere else the next time we are in Melbourne. Alyssa

With the apartment taking off and sensational reviews flying in, I knew it was time to up my rate. What did I do? I (almost) doubled the rate, and the bookings went through the roof. The apartment was the hottest piece of Airbnb real estate in town, and I was starting to welcome back guests for their second or third time. I had started out with a rate of about $120 per night and I upped it to just below $200 per night. There is nothing better than having a guest who has had such a great stay they sing your praises and say, 'I'll be back' – sometimes again and again.

Returning guests – Keep them coming back for more

I developed a connection with, and a soft spot for, many of my returning guests, and I would always look after them with an extra discount or some added goodies for their stay. I loved to spoil my guests, especially when they came back for more.

One lovely couple used to stay each January to attend the Australian Open. One year they left some jewellery behind and I sent it back to them via Express Post. They were quite taken that I had not expected them to pay for the postage and that I cared enough to follow up to see if it had arrived home safely. They were also surprised when I offered them a discount for their next stay. They were touched by my actions and couldn't wait to come and stay again. For one of their visits, I wasn't able to be around, but I made sure they were taken care of, and I received this lovely message: *Thanks so much, Juls! You are (by far) the best Airbnb host we've encountered.* Ben

Another couple who came to stay, Liz and her husband, Jonathon, were from New Zealand. They loved visiting Melbourne and going to the Formula 1, and Liz loved Melbourne's shopping culture. They were great characters, lots of fun, and were fellow Airbnb hosts so we had a laugh swapping host stories. Liz would say: *Juls, we just love coming back to your place. It is the best little apartment in town.* On one of their stays, Jonathon, a project manager, picked up that the air conditioner was not functioning very well and asked when I'd last had the filters on the heat pump cleaned. I'd had a sneaking suspicion something wasn't quite right with the air conditioner, but I wasn't too concerned. It was a good thing Jonathon raised the alarm bells, as the problem had the potential to become a far bigger issue, and I probably saved a lot of money by dealing with it there and then.

Another of my gorgeous repeat guests was a beautiful young lady visiting from the UK, Katie. Katie was so full of life. She was travelling solo around Australia, and I immediately felt protective towards her, just like an aunty, and I wanted to make sure Katie felt comfortable and secure being in a big city so far from home. She stayed for three weeks and then went travelling around Australia. At the end of her trip, she decided to come back to Melbourne as this was where she wanted to settle permanently. Katie came back to the apartment and used it as a landing pad until she found a permanent home.

Thanks so much, Juls. It's experiences like these that make me continue to use Airbnb and it was such a nice place to land while I found longer term housing. It was perfect. We need more hosts like you, Juls!

Perhaps the guest that impacted me most, was Susie, my first returning guest. Susie was one of those people who leaves an indelible mark on your life. She was one of the coolest cats I ever had stay at my apartment. Susie loved the apartment so much, that after her first stay, she decided it was to be her home away from home when she came to Melbourne for business, which was every month.

Susie was in her late fifties and had an amazing zest for life. She was a go-getter and fearless − a trail blazer. I knew from my first contact with her that she was a very special lady. She absolutely loved the apartment, and I could not have been happier to accommodate her; she was every host's dream guest.

Despite not having ever met Susie in person, we got on like a house on fire. We instantly connected through our communications on email and phone. Her passion was motorbikes. She loved them and was president of her biking club. I don't normally ingratiate myself into someone's life, but I couldn't wait to meet this powerhouse of a woman.

When Susie booked for another visit, we organised to meet and catch up for a coffee – we were finally going to make it happen. I was super excited to meet her and was in no doubt it would be a memorable catch up.

About a week before Susie's stay, I received a message from her brother. He informed me that Susie had been out on a motorbike ride with some mates and there had been a terrible accident. She had been struck by a car and killed. I couldn't believe what I was reading. I sat staring at the message with tears streaming down my face. I felt a great sadness wash over me. All deaths are sad, but for me, Susie's death was particularly impactful because I saw her as a beacon of light in this sometimes very dark world.

Susie had stayed at the apartment three times, and I had only known her through email and phone contact, but her insatiable zest for life, 'can do' attitude and youthful energy made a lasting impression on me.

Not all your guests will be perfect, but most will reflect the effort you put into your hosting.

With my guests, it felt like all my hard work had paid off. I treated my guests like royalty, and this was reflected in delicious reviews, bookings that came in thick and fast, and returning guests. I knew the apartment's worth, and I reaped the rewards – my business was a roaring success.

For me, my greatest reward was the reviews I was receiving from my guests and the knowledge that I was giving my guests a memorable experience at my apartment. Excellence is memorable.

Secret # 7: Know your worth

If you provide excellence – excellent location, an excellent property, excellent service – you can and should charge a premium. Do whatever you can to make your Airbnb better than anything else on offer, and you will be able to charge more and reap the rewards financially.

8

The Body Corporate

Keep your friends close, but your enemies closer.
Michael Corleone in *The Godfather*

When I bought my apartment in 2015, I was a little ahead of the Airbnb curve, and there were no people in my building doing Airbnb. I was wary of having to deal with other owners who might not like the idea of an Airbnb apartment in their complex. I wanted to get on the front foot and not have to deal with issues after they arose.

Adam suggested I find out who managed the owners corporation. I had never owned an apartment before, so I had absolutely no clue about the owners corporation and what it did. But, being a lawyer, Adam knew all about them.

The owners corporation (sometimes known as the body corporate) of an apartment complex manages the common property. The common property comprises the hallways, the entrance, the stairs, and any part of the property that is not privately owned. Some apartment owners do not like the idea of apartments in their complex being rented out on Airbnb. There are horror stories of apartments rented on Airbnb being used as 'party houses', where (mostly) young people rent the premises on Airbnb, have loud parties, vomit in the hallways and lifts, are continually moving in and out and cause disruption to other apartment owners.

Honesty is the best policy

As soon as the settlement on the apartment went through, I reached out to the owners corporation manager, Andrew. I let him know I was going to be running my apartment as an Airbnb. I told him I felt it was important to be upfront and honest about my plans. I wanted to make a good first impression because first impressions count.

Andrew was a bit sceptical about me running an Airbnb initially. This hadn't been done before in the building, and he didn't have any experience with Airbnb. He was naturally cautious in his approach, and I understood where he was coming from. But as I explained my plans for the Airbnb, and assured him I would run a tight ship, he warmed to the idea. I told him I was hands on, and what was very important to me was having the right clientele stay and to maintain the integrity of the apartment building and respect my neighbours. It seemed to hit the sweet spot, and he was supportive and got on board.

Tell the story

You can never go wrong when you are open and honest and 'tell the story'. People love hearing stories. Years ago, I took my son and his friend to a gaming expo that was interstate. We flew to Sydney for the weekend and had two full days at the expo. What I didn't know was that if you were under eighteen you couldn't get into the really cool gaming areas. Who knew these things? I soon realised those over eighteen 'gaming spaces' are why you go to gaming expos. That is where all the fun is, especially for a teenage boy. Who wants to just hang out in the 'G' or 'PG' areas? I realised this was going to be a pretty lame experience if the boys weren't able to access the fun pits, so I approached one of the security guys at the entrance and explained my situation. I told him 'the story'. I told him that we had come all the way from Melbourne, and the boys were really excited as this was their first gaming experience, but they couldn't go into certain areas because they were underage. I was feeling quite stressed and burst into tears (unplanned, but a nice touch all the same). The security guy said, 'No problem, ma'am, in you go.' Slam dunk. The boys had the best time because I had saved the day by telling 'the story'.

Tell your guests to respect the neighbours and they will

I am happy to say, I never had any complaints from the owners corporation (or other apartment owners) about the apartment being run as an Airbnb. As I had explained to Andrew (the owners corporation manager), I let my guests know before check-in that they would be staying in a residential apartment complex and that they needed to respect the other people in the building. Because I charged higher prices for my Airbnb compared to many other one-bedroom apartments in Melbourne's CBD, and given that I took steps to ensure I got the clientele I wanted, my guests were generally sensible people who were willing to play by the rules and respect other people.

Owners corporation committee

I was also part of the owners corporation committee (Adam's idea), and it proved to be a brilliant suggestion. Being on the committee makes a huge difference with getting support for any changes or implementations with your Airbnb. There is also the bonus of having a say in the goings-on in your apartment building and any development that might affect your Airbnb business. This can sometimes save you significant expense, as I found out when I needed my windows cleaned.

The external parts of the building are the responsibility of the owners corporation and, as my apartment was on the second floor, when the windows needed cleaning an expensive cherry-picker was required to access them. By being on the owners corporation committee I was able to convince the other committee members that all the apartment owners should share the cost of window cleaning. This saved me a considerable amount of money and was a great lesson in the value of being a member of the owners corporation committee.

Beware of the rats

That's not the only example. Being on the committee also worked in my favour when there was a 'rat invasion' in the building. This was a potential catastrophe.

The building is in a laneway right next door to a café, so you can imagine the critters could have a field day, not only in our building, but also running amok with the delicious offerings on tap in a café. I was alerted to something amiss when a guest mentioned that there was a vile odour in the foyer on the second floor. Oh dear!

I sprang into action (as I do). I couldn't contemplate my guests being 'uncomfortable', 'put out' or 'disturbed' by a foul odour. I drove to the apartment, took the lift and, to my horror, was greeted by a foul stench when I stepped out on the second floor. It was disgusting. You can imagine the potential review from some poor guest having to put up with stinking (dead) rats: *'Juls' place is fabulous – great spot, fantastic communication, but stinks to high heaven and watch out for the rats!*

Being on the owners corporation committee I had Andrew's direct contact number and we had built up a good rapport. I immediately contacted him. He told me that he was aware that rats may have made their way into the wall cavities in the building and that once inside, they could not escape. The foul smell was the stench of dead rats in the walls. After some toing and froing, I realised I needed to drive the message home – the rat situation was in danger of flying under the radar. Andrew recognised the need to do something, but not the urgency. So, I followed up the call with an email:

> *Hi Andrew … I fear the 'rat' stench dilemma is reaching biblical proportions, and I'm very concerned! We need immediate action to address this dire situation … [attached is] a letter I received in my mailbox from the next-door café owners … I'm greatly concerned about the impact this situation is having on us. I truly believe we need to do something before we all have to evacuate our homes. Look forward to hearing from you, Andrew.*
> *Juls*

You might think my email was a bit over the top. However, owners corporation managers tend to manage quite a few properties, and they have many demands made on their time (some significant, some trivial), and sometimes it's hard to get their attention and motivate them into immediate action.

Rats can do horrendous damage to a building – chewing through electrical cables and sparking fires. They can also die in the walls of the building, and when they die they decompose, giving rise to the rancid smell. The survival of my Airbnb business depended on having bums in beds, and if the situation wasn't rectified, my guests were going to be like 'rats fleeing a sinking ship' – pardon the pun.

We needed to deal with the rat incursion, and we also needed something to eradicate the rat 'pong'. I put this to Andrew and suggested we get the rats exterminated and have air freshener units installed on each floor to alleviate the stench that was wafting about the building and infiltrating the apartments.

After my email to Andrew and once I got the other committee members on board, the issue was dealt with swiftly – crisis averted. And, except for that one guest who contacted me about the smell, and who probably had a very sensitive nose like me, no other guests complained, which was nothing short of a miracle!

Secret # 8: Communicate honestly with the owners corporation and deal with any serious issues as soon as they arise

If you own an apartment in a building that is subject to an owners corporation then get on the committee. That way you are part of the building management. And, when issues arise that may adversely impact your business, deal with those issues straight away.

9

Getting Down to Business

The secret to my success is I know what I don't know, and I hire people smarter than me.

Gary Hirshberg

In one of the property courses I took, various professionals gave talks about the part they play in the property investment journey. What I took away from that course was that I needed three very important players to help me run my Airbnb well – not the butcher, the baker and the candlestick maker, but an accountant, a lawyer and a bookkeeper. This made perfect sense to me – I know my strengths and my weaknesses, and what I do not have in my bag of tricks is legal and accounting skills.

Finding a lawyer was easy – I'm married to one. But I still felt it was very important to know what was going on in my business. I do not believe in handing over all my power to anyone, not even my husband. I asked questions, lots of questions. I didn't care if I sounded like an idiot by asking a stupid question. I needed to understand what I was doing, what I was dealing with and what I was signing. That way I could always dot the i's and cross the t's.

Initially, rather than use an accountant or bookkeeper, I

tried to give the books a go myself. But, like a lot of people, I hate accounting! Nothing bores the pants off me more than Microsoft Excel spreadsheets, profit and loss statements, balance sheets and Xero. (Sorry Xero, you are a godsend, and Adam says you are the best accounting package available. I am just not excited by accounting packages.) Just the mention of Excel spreadsheets and I can feel my heart race and my throat tighten. I would rather set my hair on fire than do the accounts. In other words, accounting plus Juls equals disaster.

Fired for poor administration skills

When I was eighteen, I got a job as an administration assistant in an accountancy firm. I lasted all of two weeks before I got called into the boss's office and given the pink slip. This was the only time in my life that I have ever been fired, but I deserved it – I was bloody hopeless. All those numbers and figures confused the heck out of me.

But if you are running a tiptop business, you need to have some kind of understanding about how these things work, or, at the very least, hire a good bookkeeper, which is exactly what I did. I hired Sue, our bookkeeper, to help me with the books.

If you don't have the skills, hire a bookkeeper

You can imagine the state things were in by the time Sue was brought in; it was a train wreck. I was way behind with the accounts. But after Sue took over, the accounts ran like a well-oiled machine.

I still needed to keep track of all my Airbnb income and expenses, and I entered those details into Xero. It was still a battle to make myself do this on a regular basis, but I had to do it because Sue would hold me accountable. The more serious accounting business I left to Sue. She was brilliant at her job, and I trusted her implicitly. I was in great hands. But I still felt it was important to have a general understanding of how things worked, so Sue made sure I knew the nuts and bolts of the business.

Get to know and understand the Airbnb website

The Airbnb website is an advanced website that provides you with pretty much all the information you need to keep track of the income you generate from Airbnb, including some expenses and profit and loss. It gives you your income data each month and your Airbnb (commission) expenses. It also tells you your booking or vacancy rate. You should get to know the ins and outs of the website, as it will help you run your business efficiently, and it will help you maximise your bookings and profit.

Take, for example, guests who only want to stay for one night. I am not a fan of a one-night stay at all, but I knew when I was first getting up and running that I would have to crawl before I could walk. I had to build a reputation, and I needed bums in beds. That meant I had to initially allow for a one-night minimum stay.

Having a one-night minimum stay, especially when you start out, will maximise your possible bookings. If you have a two- or three-night minimum booking, then people looking to book accommodation for one night will not 'see' your listing as a potential place to stay when they conduct their Airbnb website search.

On the flip side, allowing guests to book your apartment for a single night is more work. You have to organise your cleaner, arrange your linen to be washed, and communicate with more guests. When you think about it in the abstract, you might not realise that having a one-night minimum would add to your workload and your costs, but believe me, it does.

When I started out, I accepted one-night stays to maximise my bookings and to get as many guests to stay in my apartment as reasonably possible. This in turn gave me reviews, which in turn generated business, which in turn helped me make a name for myself.

Once the apartment was getting regular bookings, I was able to change the minimum length of stay on the Airbnb website to something longer. I did this because one-night stays can be exhausting, and personally the return wasn't there for me. People staying in the suburbs, or the country, are likely to stay for longer than one night. But my apartment is based in the CBD, where there are lots of comings and goings, which meant a lot of people looking to stay for one night.

The return (or profit) is less on one-night stays because the cleaning fee – I charged about seventy dollars per clean – did not cover my actual cleaning costs. In other words, the cleaning service was a loss leader. My actual cleaning and laundry costs were about $100 per clean (or change over). That was the amount the cleaner charged me to clean the apartment and do the laundry. Every time I had to arrange a clean of the apartment, I would make a loss of $30 – the difference between my cost ($100) and the amount I charged the guest ($70). On this basis, longer stays are more profitable because the $30 cost is incurred only once over the entire stay.

After I paid the cleaner, drove to the apartment, paid for

parking and stocked up on supplies, I was not making a good return on one-night stays. Even though all the costs were tax deductible, for the time factor alone it was not worth it. So, I started with a one-night minimum stay, moved to a two-night minimum stay, and finally settled on a three-night minimum.

Accounting: a 'necessary evil'

As well as using the tools on the Airbnb website, I recommend you get an accounting package (Xero, for example), so you always know exactly how your business is doing. This financial information is required for taxation purposes. Also, you may need to rely on the income from your business to obtain a loan from a bank or other financial institution at some point (to buy your next Airbnb apartment, for example). In other words, if you are making $10,000 profit from your Airbnb every year, for example, then that $10,000 is likely to be taxable income. It is also likely to be income the bank will take into account when assessing your eligibility to borrow money.

While you should claim all your legitimate expenses to reduce any tax liability you may incur on account of your Airbnb business, it is better to have a profitable rather than non-profitable business. Your accounting package will help you to keep track of your profits and it will help you to convince your bank to lend you more money when you need it.

If you own the property where your Airbnb business is located, that property may increase in value over time (capital growth). But you don't necessarily want to wait until you sell the property to make money – you want to make money from your use of the property. Therefore, it is important to know if your business is cashflow positive. In other words, does the income you receive from your Airbnb business exceed the various expenses (including mortgage expenses) you incur in running the business? An accounting package will help you to answer that question and keep track of your cash flow. You can do it manually, with a pen and paper or Microsoft Excel, but for peace of mind an accounting package is the way to go.

I also set up a stand-alone bank account for my Airbnb. This makes it much easier to keep track of all the income and expenses incurred in running the business. I save electronic copies of the receipts from expenses incurred in running the business to Dropbox, and each month I enter them, along with my Airbnb income, into Xero. If you don't keep on top of this then you are going to get yourself into a bind, and if you don't have receipts, you can't (properly) claim your expenses.

You should always be involved in the business, from the smallest detail to the biggest

So, get a good software package and, if you need to, hire a bookkeeper to manage your books and an accountant to do your tax. And, make sure you comply with all your taxation and other regulatory obligations. You don't want the tax man knocking on your door.

For me, it was a must to hire good people to help me run my business well, but I also made sure I had a general understanding of the important issues. You should always be involved in the business, from the smallest to the biggest detail. Never relinquish power to the people who work for you. Hire good, smart people. Get them to do the things that are out of your area of expertise. But make sure they explain what's going on, and make sure you understand what is happening with your business. Hire people who are smarter than you, as that is good business. But it's equally important to trust and back yourself and ask lots of questions.

Secret # 9: Build your Airbnb team

You can't be an expert in everything, and you don't have time to do everything. Hire people with specialist skills – lawyer, accountant, bookkeeper – and run your business like a business.

10

The Road to Superhost

I've learned that people will forget what you said, people will forget what you did, but people will never forget how you made them feel.

Maya Angelou

Three months after launching my Airbnb, it was time for my first Superhost assessment. When I set up my business, my goal was to become a Superhost – the pinnacle of Airbnb success and an outcome that most Airbnb hosts would love to achieve.

Whether you become an Airbnb Superhost largely depends on the reviews you receive from your guests. If you get excellent reviews almost all of the time (and tick a few more boxes), then you will get your Superhost badge, which will be displayed on your Airbnb listing. That means your listing will stand out from the crowd. In fact, some people limit their Airbnb search to Superhost properties when looking for a place to stay (I do this most of the time), knowing the property has a high rating and that the host will be responsive.

As you may have noticed, I bang on and on about reviews. This is because we are influenced by reviews. Think about it for a moment. You are going on a holiday and you are searching through the Airbnb listings for a place to stay. You come across a place you love the look of and check the reviews. They are out of this world. Just sensational. You immediately want to have the experience other people have raved about, and so you book that Airbnb. However, if the photos look great but the reviews are average, or there are one or two that are not very positive, you will think twice about booking that Airbnb.

When I am looking to stay at an Airbnb, I make the decision by reading the reviews. They immediately tell me what other people are saying about the place. The reviews tell me what I need to know. How was the experience for the guest? What did they enjoy? What did the host offer at their Airbnb? How did the host measure up? What service will I be getting? Why did the host get five stars?

To be a Superhost, these are the types of reviews you should be aiming for, each and every time:

Perfect host. Perfect apartment. Perfect location. Best Airbnb host and experience I've had. Harry

Juls' place is a stylish cool and really pleasant place in central Melbourne that has everything right at hand. It's the third time I've had an extended stay in the CBD and it is by far the best I've stayed in. Five star all around. Comfy bed, all the things you need for a good stay. Great place, thank you, Juls! Gabriel

Juls is a very friendly host who communicated clearly and

accurately. Her apartment totally deserves 5 stars and it is so wonderful. The apartment was extremely clean and we enjoyed the various amenities that she provided for us. We would highly recommend this to travellers. Thank you for the awesome stay! Emmanuel

I don't normally give 5-star reviews, but this Airbnb deserves it. The apartment is lovely and the location is great! Juls was really communicative through my whole stay and made herself available at all times. The apartment was really clean, and I thought everything in it was high quality, from the towels, bed sheets, mattress and even bath soap. :)) I will definitely be back and would recommend it to other travellers! Much better than a hotel. Thanks, Juls! Illeana

Become a Superhost and reap the rewards

Given that guests can expect to have a fantastic experience at a Superhost property, the Superhost can charge a premium for that privilege. Accordingly, if you wish to maximise your profits, you should make becoming a Superhost one of your goals.

I wanted to receive five-star reviews from every guest who stayed at my Airbnb, and I am proud to say I came very close to achieving that goal. And because I was consistently getting five-star reviews, I could justify listing my apartment for a higher rate than the average apartment available in Melbourne at the time. People did not complain about the price because the experience I gave my guests met or exceeded their expectations. Perception is everything and this is why your reviews mean everything. If you deliver excellence each time, every time, then your guests will not forget. They will tell the world about their experience and they'll keep coming back. Excellence is unforgettable.

Reviews, reviews, reviews

When buying and selling real estate, it is always a question of: 'Location, location, location.' In other words, it is the location that will largely determine the property's price. You can have the worst house in the best street, and people will still want to buy your home because of the location. With Airbnb, it is all about, 'Reviews, reviews, reviews'. Without a doubt, those words describing your guest's stay are going to make the difference between your Airbnb getting booked only some of the time or getting booked out (virtually) all of the time.

To be a Superhost, you need to give your guests an 'out of this world' stay at your Airbnb.

The outstanding reviews I got time after time were my key to having near full capacity with my Airbnb listings. It didn't matter that Joe Bloggs down the road had their Airbnb $30 to $40 dollars per night cheaper, my five-star reviews meant that people wanted to stay at my Airbnb.

Reviews paint a picture of the Airbnb, the location and you, the host, and they tell the story of the experience the guest had. If the story told by the reviewer is a magnificent one, the next guest will be very eager to have that experience too.

Don't underestimate the power of a review. They are impactful whether they are negative or positive. They are also valuable feedback to you, giving you insight into what guests enjoyed about their stay and how you are doing as a host.

Awesome apartment, very clean and in a perfect location. Juls is very helpful and friendly, overall a 5/5 and would recommend to anyone! Jack

A home away from home

If receiving excellent reviews is the key to the Superhost kingdom, then the next question is, how do you get excellent reviews? To be a Superhost, you need to give your guests an 'out of this world' stay at your Airbnb – a memorable 'home away from home' experience. To do this requires at least two things. First, you need a special place, and that doesn't just mean the property, it includes all the little extras. Second, you need to communicate with and help your guests when they need it. You need to go the extra mile for your guests – promise and deliver.

Had just an amazing time staying at the apartment! Juls was a great host and went above and beyond with her communication and extras for our stay! Can't compliment her more! The apartment was in a perfect location. Will definitely stay again. Claudia

Whatever you promise, make sure you deliver

I once stayed in an apartment that was promoted as 'Five-star, luxury accommodation'. As the advert stated, 'luxury accommodation', that was what I was expecting – to be staying in luxury. I don't know what planet the host was on, but five-star luxury accommodation it was not.

From the outset there were issues. The instructions on how to collect the keys were a riddle, and after 30 minutes of trying to locate the collection point, I was left waiting for someone to come and attend to me. Hmm, not a great start. After I checked into the apartment, the surprises kept coming. The kitchen was bare. Apart from some tea and coffee sachets and a few pots and pans that should have been put in the garbage bin years ago, it was a very sad and lonely room. The freezer had such a massive build-up of ice that you couldn't put any food in it, and the fridge had water leaking from underneath. The microwave didn't work, and there wasn't even dishwashing liquid to do the dishes. Some light globes needed replacing. The pillows were lumpy, and the doonas had no doona covers. What is it with no doona covers?

The host wasn't very helpful when I raised the issues. 'Oh yes,' he said. 'I am aware of these things. I'll get to them when you leave.' Wrong answer. These things have an impact on your stay. What if I had slipped on the water leaking from the fridge? I could have been seriously injured. When I mentioned there was no doona cover on the bed, he simply said they don't use doona covers. I told him I was a host myself, and I would be horrified if one of my guests was experiencing what I was having to put up with. It just wasn't good enough.

Go the extra mile: provide the little extras

Once upon a time, not providing basic supplies was acceptable. These days that doesn't fly – certainly not if you want to be a Superhost. You are not a motel, a hotel, a bed and breakfast or a serviced apartment. Your guests are not going on a camping trip where they expect to have to take all their supplies. You are part of the Airbnb family, and in my opinion, Airbnb is a 'home away from home' experience. Every so often, there will be a guest who has forgotten their toothbrush or razor or deodorant. I supplied those items at my Airbnb. And when a guest needed them (very rarely) they were very happy to see I had thought to provide these little things. If you go the extra mile, you will be rewarded tenfold.

A beautiful apartment in a great location AND very quiet – lovely … Very nicely appointed, and I particularly love the thoughtfulness Juls showed supplying things that I would not have had time to get myself arriving as late as I did. I am booked to come back several more times this month. My little haven in the CBD. Thank, Juls. Aidan

A small investment to multiply your bookings

If you are wondering why you should spend your money providing plunger coffee, cooking oil, spare razors, a spare toothbrush and deodorant, my answer is simple: your guests will love the fact that you surpass their expectations, they will give you a rave review and they will come back. Just think about it for a moment: you are on a business trip and you forget your toiletries. You look in the bathroom cupboard at the Airbnb and your prayers are answered. The host will receive both a rave review and a guest who will want to return. Rave reviews generate more bookings, and the

Your guests will love the fact you surpass their expectations.

money you spend on the little extras will be a drop in the ocean compared to the money you generate from repeat business and your high occupancy rate.

I ended up being given Superhost on my first assessment – not a bad effort for having only been an Airbnb host for three months. It was a very proud moment for me. But I wanted to hold onto that Superhost status, and that meant being assessed every three months. When the second assessment came around, I received this note from Airbnb:

Congratulations, Juls,

You did it again! You've been a Superhost now for 2 quarters. In the year leading up to 2016-03-31, you qualified by hosting 55 trips and earning 5-star reviews 93% of the time. Your response rate was 100% with no cancellations.

You've delighted and supported your guests, and we think that deserves to be rewarded.

A guest book for personal written reviews

It was a pattern that continued; I achieved Superhost status on every assessment that followed. Great reviews aren't just important for maintaining your Airbnb Superhost status, ensuring you get constant bookings and making your Airbnb a financial success, they are also important for bringing you joy as an Airbnb host. I had one set of reviews that gave me a great amount of joy, but which were never posted on Airbnb and didn't count towards my Superhost status – I had a guest book, where guests could leave handwritten reviews. These messages are particularly special to me as they are a tangible reminder of the joy and happiness my guests experienced at my Airbnb.

Receiving a handwritten message from a guest is very different from reading an online review. It is much like receiving a letter in the post from a friend, rather than reading their post on Facebook. When our children, Alec and Paris, were young,

Adam and I sent them to summer camp in Raymond, Maine in the USA. Adam had been a summer camp counsellor when he was twenty-one and was very keen for our kids to attend summer camp as campers. When Alec was all of twelve years old, we put him on a plane on his own, and off he went to the USA for seven weeks. Paris was only ten years old when she had her first summer camp experience. The camps helped them build resilience and independence. They also gave them a gift for letter writing.

When you arrive at summer camp you have to relinquish all your electronic devices and can only contact your parents by writing letters to them. So, when Alec and Paris were at camp, they wrote letters home, and Adam and I wrote letters back to them. This was fantastic. I hadn't been so excited to see what was in my letterbox since I was a kid myself. I would eagerly rip open each envelope and devour the letter. I could feel their emotions from their writing. I could tell if they were happy or if they were feeling a bit homesick. I could sense their excitement.

It was the same when I read the handwritten reviews from my Airbnb guests. There was something very special about picking up the guest book and reading the heartfelt messages the guests had written on the pages.

THANK YOU for everything. You are Airbnb Royalty. Jeff, California USA

We have stayed in many Airbnb's all over the world, and I agree with a previous comment, that you are 'Airbnb Royalty'. Mandy and Marcus, Freemantle, Western Australia

I was very emotional when I read these two reviews. I felt like the blood, sweat and tears I had invested into Airbnb and my guests was encapsulated in those two words 'Airbnb Royalty'. To read that people regarded me so highly and that their experience had been so rewarding for them was incredibly moving. And being handwritten, made them especially important to me.

Best place we have stayed in OZ so far. Emma and Dan, London

Again, I was humbled to know my guests loved their stay at my Airbnb. Their words reinforced that I was doing a good job.

Thank you, Juls! ... Your attention to detail was five star. Thank you! Ed, Toronto, Canada

All my attention to detail and fastidiousness, including arriving at the apartment at 5 am on some occasions to make sure everything was perfect for my next guests, was being validated.

Wow! What a hidden gem ... Juls your kindness and help has made this feel like a 'home away from home'. Jill and Patrick

Communication, attention to all the little extra details was so welcome and helped to make this our best ever AIRBNB experience. Robbie and Maria, New Zealand

Love, love, love your apartment! Created with love, we felt at home. Your taste is impeccable, but there's something more at work here … the feeling of warmth extends to all those who require a 'home', not just accommodation. Stacey

You've thought of everything – not once did we have a need that you hadn't catered for. Nanette and Andy

We love everything about your place. You've thought of everything. We do appreciate your attention to detail. You are a true superhost. Jane and Steve, USA

It was not only lovely to receive personal, handwritten reviews from guests, it also helped me understand how my Airbnb was doing and if anything needed tweaking. By asking guests to give their input, I could make their stay more comfortable, make them feel valued and show that I cared about them and their opinion. So don't think that a guestbook is outdated. It is still as effective today as it was many years ago.

Thanks for the opportunity to stay at the loveliest Airbnb apartment ever. Stephanie, Singapore

I have been blown away and humbled by the reviews I received from my guests. Most were heart warming and many were incredibly moving! When I was sifting through the reviews to choose the ones I wanted to include in this book, I was overcome with emotion. I don't usually like having a spotlight on me, and so it was really the first time I had sat down and read the reviews carefully. I was filled with gratitude. It was a wonderful feeling, and you can experience it too. Go the extra mile, ensure your guests are comfortable and that they have a memorable stay, and you will get the rewards.

> *WOW! What an apartment. Located in the heart of the CBD, though with a warm and welcoming vibe. Juls' apartment had exceeded all expectations and she truly is a 'superhost' – more than accommodating. This will be my first choice of accommodation in Melbourne.* Shay-Lee

Secret # 10: Reviews are the currency of Airbnb

Go the extra mile and you will reap the rewards. Provide a memorable experience and your guests will reward you with great reviews and so much more. If you consistently get five-star reviews, you achieve Superhost status and your Airbnb becomes even more desirable. Don't devalue your currency by receiving second-rate reviews. Excellence is unforgettable.

11

Back to School Again

The more that you read, the more things you will know.
The more that you learn, the more places you'll go.

Dr Seuss

Now that my Airbnb had been in operation for a while, it was time to look again at the second course I was interested in. This was an interactive course that went into the nitty-gritty of running an Airbnb. It covered topics such as cleaners, tax, insurance, owners corporation and house manual.

This course was the GuestReady 'Kickstarter Program'. Jodie Wilmer, the owner of GuestReady, ran the course. She had put it together to help newcomers get the most valuable knowledge on how to run an Airbnb. Like me, she was a top Airbnb host and shared her experiences during the personal one-on-one sessions I had with her. It was the perfect way to learn. Jodie was organised, her course was well structured, and she was the best person to help me hone my Airbnb skills and increase my Airbnb knowledge. The little things I picked up were invaluable, and I have no doubt that without this course I would have made lots of mistakes along the way.

Get the right insurance

One mistake I found I'd made was with the type of insurance I'd chosen. When I started operating my Airbnb, I assumed I needed to take out good old standard landlord insurance. I had no idea there are several landlord insurances on offer: property management insurance, landlord preferred self-managed insurance, long-term rental insurance, and short-term holiday rental insurance.

Initially I had my apartment insured with a long-term rental insurance policy, because I assumed that was the right insurance for what I was doing. I knew I needed landlord insurance and assumed it was one size fits all. Little did I know that I had taken out the wrong one.

During the course with Jodie, she asked whether I had short-term accommodation or holiday insurance. I told her I didn't have either; I had insured my apartment under a long-term rental policy. Jodie explained the different types of landlord insurance and told me I had the wrong policy and may not be covered if I needed to make a claim. No-one at the insurance company had shared that information with me. They just signed me up and that was that. Never 'assume' as you will 'make an ass out of u and me'! Thank God it was easy-peasy changing to the right insurance.

Unfortunately, it wasn't the first insurance mistake I have made. Years ago, Adam got a job interstate. We uprooted our lives, rented out our home in Melbourne and moved. For some bizarre reason I ended up with two insurance policies on our house. I had absolutely no idea I had two policies, but I did. (You see why I need good administrative-type people around me rather than being left to my own devices?) The only reason I found this out was because our house in Melbourne was broken into while it was vacant and there was some damage. We needed to get the damage fixed before we could re-let the property. When I contacted the insurance company, they alerted me to the fact that I had two policies and because of that they told me I would not be able to claim for insurance.

Luckily for us, Adam had done a stint with a company as an in-house lawyer and had worked in their disputes department, so he knew how to deal with the situation. Most people don't have the luxury of having a lawyer in the family and would most likely accept the insurance company's 'denial of liability'. We ended up getting a positive result, but it was an uphill battle.

My advice is to do your research and make sure you talk to your insurance company about the right insurance policy for your Airbnb. And read through the policy carefully to check what it does and does not cover – the devil is always in the detail.

Thanks to Jodie, I was able to change to the correct type of policy before I needed to make a claim. My investment in learning paid off.

Secret # 11: Invest in your Airbnb education

Read, watch, listen, talk – the more time and money you invest in learning about Airbnb, the more successful you will be. Start when you are first thinking about setting up an Airbnb – you want great reviews from the moment you open your doors – and then keep learning. Take a course, read a book or learn the tricks of the trade from another host.

12

The Cleaner

Housework can't kill you, but why take a chance.
Phyllis Diller

I had no interest or desire to clean my Airbnb apartment, but for the first two months I did the cleaning and laundry myself. Schlepping about town with my mop, bucket and cleaning products did my back no favours, but it was the best thing I could have done; I got to know my apartment from top to bottom. I found all the little places that can be missed. And, by doing it myself in the early days, I knew what I needed from a cleaner.

Cleaning is a considerable expense, and for that reason a lot of people who operate an Airbnb business choose to do it themselves. However, it wasn't the best option for me.

While I was doing the cleaning, I had been getting great reviews about the cleanliness of the apartment.

Thanks, Juls, the title 'home away from home' is very appropriate. The apartment was extremely clean and welcoming, and the little touches of some basics in the fridge and pantry were very much appreciated. Look forward to booking again soon. Ross

Find a good cleaner

Finding someone equally good to do the cleaning would be no easy feat. It almost goes without saying that cleanliness is important. Your guests will not always compliment you for having a spotless shower or a floor they could eat off, but they will say something if you drop the ball, and they find your Airbnb is dirty when they arrive. And if a prickly guest finds hair in the bathtub, a bad review may be on its way. So, I needed to find someone reliable and trustworthy, someone I could call upon when needed, and who would get the job done to my liking. I didn't want to risk getting a bad review because the apartment wasn't cleaned properly.

Initially I advertised on the Airbnb Community Board. It's a great place to start, as people who clean Airbnbs work differently to your average residential cleaner. I had a few bites, but no-one really jumped out at me.

As luck would have it, I found my cleaner, Sharon, through a referral from Jodie who ran the GuestReady 'Kickstarter Program'. Sharon was her cleaner, and Jodie was very happy with her.

Sharon exuded warmth and I felt comfortable with her. Plus, she was already cleaning Airbnb accommodation and knew the drill. I felt like I had hit the jackpot.

I soon developed a great relationship with Sharon that extended past her simply doing the cleaning. I was able to rely on her to be my contact person for the guests when I went away. She knew the apartment inside and out, and I could be confident my guests were in safe hands if anything went awry. So, when a holiday email popped up in my inbox soon after she started working for me, I didn't immediately delete it.

The holiday was a sixteen-day trek to Everest Base Camp in Nepal. Before Adam's cancer, I would not have given it a second thought. But after what we had been through, it piqued my interest. The previous year, Nepal had experienced a serious earthquake. The country was very keen for the tourists to return and, despite the risk, this was something I thought that we (the family) needed to do.

Adam's periodic check-ups had been clear, apart from one scare when the doctors suspected the cancer had got into his bones. If by some chance the cancer did return, then what an experience this Nepal trip could be for Adam, and for us as a family. I wasn't even thinking about the implications of the kids being so young. I just thought this was a once in a lifetime experience.

Without thinking twice, I pressed the 'Buy now' button. I had just bought us a sixteen-day trek to Everest Base Camp. I must admit I went from euphoria to panic pretty quickly. What have I done? Am I crazy? How will Adam and the kids react?

In my heart, I knew the cancer could come back – that Adam could die. Adam loves adventure, and I thought that if that was his fate, then this would be the adventure of a lifetime. Doing it together as a family – now that would be something.

Hiring Sharon not only allowed me to go on holiday, it also freed up my time so that I could be more productive. In my case, paying $100 for the cleaning and laundering (linen, not money) was a no-brainer. For starters I could claim it as a tax deduction, and it was a lot cheaper to pay Sharon than to pay for a professional service to look after my Airbnb when I was away. Don't scrimp on the small things, is my advice. Besides, if you do the cleaning yourself (and if you are like me and not a natural born cleaner) you may end up resenting your Airbnb business.

With Airbnb, you need a cleaner who is able to clean at the drop of a hat. Whether a guest is staying one night, three nights or two weeks, the accommodation needs to be cleaned so the cleaner has to be able to slot in at pretty much any time. Airbnb has a great tool on its website that allows you to sync your Airbnb calendar with your cleaner's calendar so they know exactly when to go in and clean your Airbnb.

If you do the cleaning yourself, you may end up resenting your Airbnb business.

Because your cleaner may not be available all the time, it is a good idea to invest in two cleaners so that you have a back-up. As Sharon had a team of cleaners who worked for her, I didn't feel it necessary to hire another cleaner. If someone was ill, Sharon would call upon one of her other cleaners to do the job, or she would do it herself.

If you are relying on one cleaner and they pull the pin at the eleventh hour, you can be left in quite a bind. There is nothing worse than having a guest arriving in a couple of hours, and your cleaner calls in sick, leaving you with an Airbnb that isn't ready. What are your options? Contact a cleaning company to do a last minute clean? They won't know the Airbnb protocol or have knowledge of how the Airbnb process works. Clean the apartment yourself? If you have done it before then you'll know the drill; and while it won't be fun, at least you can get it done.

Try to think of all scenarios that could (and will) happen. It was lucky for me that Sharon had a team of cleaners. But I am not immune from bad luck and unforeseen events, and on occasion I had to drop everything and hightail it to the apartment and do the cleaning myself.

Cleaning and laundry combined

I also recommend hiring a cleaner who does the laundry. That way you can kill two birds with one stone. Sharon cleaned and also changed the linen and towels. I had two sets of towels and two sets of linen, and Sharon kept the spare set, switched them over when cleaning and laundered the used set. It was so much easier than me having to wash the linen and towels myself, or having a different service for the laundry.

If you have a good relationship with your cleaner, ask them to do a check through of your apartment from time to time, to see how everything is working, what needs fixing and if anything needs upgrading (such as the mattress). And it's always wise to stay at your Airbnb occasionally yourself, to see it from the perspective of your guests. You could even get a friend or family member to stay overnight. (There are so many ways to skin a cat!) You want your apartment in tiptop shape all the time.

Stay at your Airbnb occasionally, and see it from the perspective of your guests.

Secret # 12: Hire a good cleaner

Having a good cleaner, someone you can trust, is important. Ask your cleaner to do the laundry (change the bedding and towels) as well. Even if you mostly do the cleaning yourself, it's a good idea to have a cleaner you can call on if you need to. Your cleaner may become an important part of your Airbnb operation.

13

You Can't Win 'Em All

The smallest act of kindness is worth more than the greatest intention.

Khalil Gibram

When I first embarked on the Airbnb journey, I said to myself, 'Juls, what do *you* want when you stay in Airbnb accommodation? What ticks your boxes?'

I came up with a list that included a comfortable bed and nice pillows, easy check-in, decent coffee, milk in the fridge, and a nice hot shower. But not everyone is me. We are all very different people. Some guests love their creature comforts – a luxurious bed and a blissful shower. For others, it's the little things, like a bottle of wine on arrival and freshly ground coffee. Some guests won't care so much about the little things, what is important for them is that the accommodation is quiet, with no outside noise to disturb them, or that the Airbnb has dark curtains, so the sun doesn't come shining through at six o'clock to wake them. I tried to cover these various needs, and the guests appreciated it.

One bad review can tarnish your well-earned reputation.

The flat is exactly as described and pictured in the photos and listing. The location is perfect and super central on a small quiet lane. We were there over New Year's Eve and although there is a small bar on the lane directly opposite the apartment the noise was minimal, due to the effective double glazing and window shutters. We slept well in the superbly comfortable bed. Fantastic eateries are located in the actual lane and immediate vicinity. Access to Netflix was a great touch and managed to catch up with missing episodes of Homeland! The host Juls was very informative and professional, timely answering all the many questions that we posed to her. We would not hesitate to recommend this apartment and host to fellow travellers. Ricci and Judy

When problems occur respond promptly and try to find a solution

My apartment is in the city of Melbourne; the hustle and bustle of the city is part of the fabric – so are construction works. And one guest, Barry, who was particularly sensitive to noise, was not happy.

Flat great/cool but disappointing that we weren't made aware of major construction works next door. Drilling started 7am this morning so no sleep in.
Barry

I immediately responded with:

Hi Barry,
I'm so sorry to hear that. The building works have been going

for about 18 months and we have never had a complaint from any guest. Maybe they are ramping the works up. I am not sure but I will look into it. I know there are a plethora of building works happening in the CBD as infrastructure is growing at such a rapid rate. There are ear plugs in the basket in the cupboard above the fridge and some in the bathroom (two different types), which may help and please let me know if there's anything else I can do.
Cheers
Juls

The next day, I followed up.

Hi Barry,
Just checking in to see how you slept last night? I hope the ear plugs helped. I did some digging and unfortunately building works in the CBD on a weekday can kick off at 7 am. No-one has raised the early works issue before so please let me know if they are continuing to cause disruption. I'm really sorry you have had not had a pleasant first night. I can only hope yesterday was a great day. I look forward to hearing how it's going.
Cheers
Juls

And Barry replied.

No dramas. 7 am start again today but I think our ears are getting used to it. The flat is great and very comfortable.
Barry

It was important for Barry to know I was trying to deal with the annoying early morning construction noise and would do all I could to get to the bottom of the issue. Construction work started at 7 am, and I wasn't in a position to control that situation. But what I could do was take the necessary steps to find out what the construction hours were and see what I could do to help make Barry's stay more comfortable. By making this small gesture, it showed Barry I had made an effort, which appeased him. He was then able to relax and enjoy the remainder of his stay. Guests are generally reasonable people. If you have a complaint from a guest about a matter that is out of your control, and you respond and explain the situation in a timely fashion, your guests are likely to accept the situation.

Another guest, Frank, claimed he was kept awake by noise going on around the building. He sent me a message after his first night at the apartment saying there was construction work next door and the builders worked all through the night – he was very unhappy.

With building work of any sort in the City of Melbourne, the builders have to notify the occupants of the apartment block and must send a letter out to all adjacent buildings to let people know they are doing night works. I was straight onto it, and I told Frank I would investigate and get back to him. I also reminded him that there were ear plugs provided in case there was noise at night.

Being in the centre of Melbourne, guests could expect there might be some noise from people leaving bars and nightclubs, but Frank was not expected to put up with excess noise. I was determined to get to the bottom of it, but if I couldn't solve the problem, I would happily refund his stay if he wanted to vacate.

First, I contacted the local council. They were very helpful and informed me there should not be any night works going on. Just because there were lights on at a building site at night, it did not always mean there were actual works going on. If there were, the building company would have to get a special permit. The person I spoke to said it would most likely be roadworks. Roadworks were under the jurisdiction of VicRoads. I contacted VicRoads and they could not find any works going on at that time. I was then told to get in touch with the Metro Tunnel project managers. At the time there was a tunnel being constructed under the city, and it involved periods of night work – information I had put in the communications I sent out to all my guests at the time, as I didn't want them to have unexpected shocks. I checked the email messages I was receiving from Metro Tunnels each week outlining the work being carried out and notifying me of any night works; there was no night work scheduled in the vicinity of the apartment.

The council also gave me a contact number for after-hours security. They said I could contact security at any time during the night, and security would go to the building site and investigate. I let Frank know what was happening, which was that 'nothing should be happening'. He seemed satisfied with my investigations and said he would let me know if there was any more construction work going on that night.

Frank contacted me at midnight that evening and said they were at it again. I wanted to get this sorted for him, so I called the night security number the council had given me. They investigated and got back to me in the wee hours of the morning with assurances there were no works going on at that building site.

I tried to contact Frank, but I never heard back from him. Frank was gone, and he had written a pretty defamatory review (complete with profanity) about me and my apartment. I contacted Airbnb about his review and they investigated. They were not impressed with Frank's allegations and foul language, and took his review down.

So, you see, despite your best efforts to resolve a situation, sometimes those efforts will not work. Unfortunately, one bad review can tarnish your well-earned reputation and has the potential to bring you down. I am very grateful that Airbnb saw the situation for what it was and acted immediately to remove Frank's critical and unseemly review. My reputation was left intact.

Be aware, you are not immune to bad press from your guests, and no matter what you do, you'll never be able to make one hundred per cent of your guests happy one hundred per cent of the time. But if you do the right thing by your guests, responses like Frank's will be the exception, and most of your reviews will be like this:

Juls made our first Airbnb experience so positive. Excellent communication, the apartment had everything we needed and the location was perfect, so perfect we didn't take advantage of all the creature comforts inside as we made the most of all the restaurants and cafés right outside. Juls' apartment is very quiet, modern and cosy, and we can't wait to return! Thanks again. Lara

Secret # 13: Always respond to complaints or concerns promptly and do your best to fix them

If you cannot fix the problem (stopping early morning construction works for example), then explain the situation and offer a fair and reasonable solution (ear plugs or a refund if it's really bad). If you respond promptly, explain, and offer a work around, most guests will be understanding.

14

Boundary Lines

The art of being a good guest is to know when to leave.

Prince Phillip

Although I desperately wanted to satisfy all my guests and cater to everyone's needs, I came to realise I couldn't accommodate every request, and it was better to tell people how things would be. People like to be directed – a valuable lesson I learned when I was the team manager for my daughter's local weekend tennis competition.

As team manager, one of my duties was to compile the roster for each competition. This was not a straightforward exercise, as anybody who has been a manager for their kid's sports team would attest to. Before I put together each roster, I would send out an email to the parents requesting dates their child would be unavailable to play.

There was one family that made my life hell. Nearly every Saturday night, I would get an email saying, 'Sorry, Juls, Abbie can't play tomorrow morning, she is unwell,' or 'Sorry, Juls, Abbie can't play tomorrow morning, there is a basketball clash.' Sometimes these emails would come in after midnight!

Initially, I tried to be understanding of this 'dilemma', but I quickly realised this person was not 'getting it'. Adam said to me, 'Juls, you need to be assertive and take control of the situation.'

By that stage, I'd had a gutful of this behaviour, so I took his advice and sent a group email stating it was unacceptable to notify me at the eleventh hour if a child couldn't play. I would be understanding if it was an emergency, but I would report repeat offenders to the club president, and if it continued the child would be pulled from the team. Miraculously, the child in question turned up every week after that.

House rules

If you tell people how things are going to be, they get on board and are happy to take your lead. Rather than leaving it up to my guests to make all the decisions, I let them know the lay of the land and gave them a set of house rules.

People respect someone who shows confidence and gives clarity. I never had a major problem with any guest because I was assertive and set the ground rules. People are much happier if they have clear guidelines. If you tell them how the system works and what they can and can't do, most people will do the right thing.

People are much happier if they have clear guidelines.

One boundary I learnt to set was with guests who suggested meeting up for a coffee or a glass of wine. Some hosts really enjoy this process, but I didn't. I am not a meet and greet kind of gal, and that is why I had self-check-ins – it worked perfectly. I was happy to assist guests when they needed help, and I wanted them to enjoy their stay, but meet and greets weren't for me.

When I started out, I would meet guests if they really

wanted me to, as I felt this was something I should do rather than wanted to do. I felt a sense of obligation. I have stayed at Airbnbs where the host loves to meet and have a chat, which is wonderful if that is your preference, but for me this wasn't something I wanted as an Airbnb host. The time commitment in meeting and greeting is significant, and for me that was a bridge too far.

As a host, you also have to be careful not to impose yourself on your guests. I once stayed at an Airbnb where the host lived close by, and he kept coming over to check on how we were. It got to the point where I would pretend I wasn't there if I saw him coming down the driveway.

If you are offering a room in your home or you live onsite you may be in regular contact with your guests, but I specifically set up my apartment as a self-check-in so I wouldn't have to meet anyone. I would send the building and apartment codes by email and text about 24 hours before check-in. This system worked like a charm.

If you really don't want to meet and greet or catch up for a vino or coffee, then don't. This is your business, so run it how you want to. If I had met every guest who wanted to meet me, I would have spent half my time having coffees and wine with people. Trust me, you won't hurt anyone's feelings by respectfully declining. I have it in my advertisement that I am not available to meet people. This didn't hurt my business one little bit. All you do is set the boundaries from the outset.

Luggage storage

Another boundary I had to set related to luggage, as guests frequently asked if they could leave their luggage after check-out and collect it later in the day. Usually this was because they had a late flight to catch and they wanted to be able to walk about town luggage-free.

Once again, in the early days I accommodated such requests as best I could. I would allow the guests to leave their luggage and come back and collect it by a set time (usually 12.30 pm as other guests would be checking in at 2 pm), but it just made life way too complicated. It meant Sharon or one of her cleaners often had to work around luggage, which wasn't always packed. At times, the cleaners arrived to find the guests hadn't even vacated the apartment, and they were still sitting there with their bags unpacked. This resulted in some guests overlapping with the new guests arriving, especially if the new guests unexpectedly turned up early. The last thing you want is guests crossing over. So, while in the early days I did allow luggage storage, after a couple of luggage incidents, I changed the rules and generally did not permit luggage storage.

There are many luggage storage services around, so don't be afraid to tell people about them. I made it a point to put links to some local luggage storage services in my apartment manual. I found that if I directed guests to alternate storage options, they were happy to take up the suggestion. (I have included a copy of the apartment manual I used for my Airbnb at the back of this book, just after the checklists).

Early check-in, late check-out

The most frequent requests I received from guests were for early check-ins and late check-outs. If I had no-one staying at the apartment the day of a guest's arrival, I would allow an earlier check-in. At the other end of the stay, if a guest asked to check-out late, I would do my very best to give them the latest possible check-out time. I really would bend over backwards to accommodate these requests.

I understand why people ask; I do it myself. If you don't ask, you don't get. The difference is, when I request an early check-in or late check-out, I listen to what the host has told me. If the host says I can check-in at 12 pm, then I will check-in at 12 pm, not 10 am. If the host says I can check-out late but will need to have my bags packed and left out of the way so the cleaner can clean the room, I will make sure I do that. Or if the host says I may drop my bags off early, but I will have to come back at such and such a time because the room needs to be cleaned, I will do what is asked. But as I found out, you can create a rod for your own back if you are too accommodating, because some people just don't listen, which gave me a lot of headaches.

Working around unreasonable guests

One day, early on as a host, I was at the apartment cleaning and in walked a couple with a baby. This was 9.30 am. Check-in was 2.00 pm. 'Can I help you,' I said (even though I knew exactly who they were). 'Oh, you're very early. Check-in is at 2 pm.' They said they had arrived early and decided to check-in. All the time I am staring at them and thinking, I have a no baby/child policy. (The reason I had a no-child policy was because the apartment had a balcony, and I didn't want a young child opening the balcony door and an accident happening.) They said not to worry about them being there and that I could keep cleaning around them. They weren't bothered in the slightest that this was creating an unnecessary headache and assumed it was fine to check-in when they wanted. What if there had been other guests staying at the apartment who had not yet checked out? Check-out is at 10 am, and guests are often in the apartment until that time. How would it have looked if these people had rocked up and checked themselves in while the previous guests were still in the apartment?

I felt like saying, 'Bugger off. The check-in time is 2 pm, and I will see you then.' However, I held my tongue and told them to leave their bags, go downstairs and have a coffee, and I would call them when I was finished cleaning. If you want to be a Superhost, you have to be accommodating and flexible, even in the face of unreasonable guests who arrive early and unannounced.

They weren't the only guests to arrive in town early and check themselves in. Because I have keyless entry and give out a code twenty-four hours before check-in, some guests assume they can check-in at their convenience. They then complain if the apartment isn't cleaned despite their early arrival. Unless you are firm with people and really spell it out for them, they will hear what they want to hear and do what they want to do. My advice is to keep it clear and simple.

One couple totally blew me away. They arrived in town early after flying in from overseas and took it upon themselves to turn up at the apartment and check themselves in well before check-in time.

I arrived at the apartment mid-morning, to make sure everything was ready for their scheduled arrival at 2 pm. You can imagine my surprise when I opened the door and discovered the couple flopped down on the couch, with the contents of their bags spread out all over the lounge room floor. They had clearly settled in for the long haul, and they weren't going anywhere. I was stunned and nearly burst out crying. I was tired of people taking advantage of my kindness. And these guests hadn't even asked for an early check-in.

The couple proceeded to let me know me they had told Sharon (my cleaner) to come back at 3 pm because they were jet lagged from their trip and wanted a nap. They then started telling me what they would like in the apartment and asked me to go out and buy some washing powder as they wanted to wash their clothes.

Under normal circumstances, I would have had time to check over the apartment and replenish any items that were low or had run out before the guests arrived (like washing powder). I was speechless. I was standing in the doorway, still holding onto the door handle, with my mouth wide open, trying to take in what I was witnessing. Their sheer arrogance flawed me. As with the couple with the baby, I wondered what they would have done if guests were still in the apartment. I have no doubt they would have just plonked themselves down on the couch and said, 'That's okay, honey, you can pack up around us.' It was sheer luck there wasn't anyone staying at the apartment the night before.

I really wanted to tell them to leave, but I knew I had to pick my battles, and this was best left alone. There was no point saying anything because they just wouldn't get it. They had absolutely no awareness of the inappropriateness of their behaviour and no respect for me as their Airbnb host. So, I put on my Juls charm and, with all the positive energy I could muster, said, 'Did you ask for an early check-in? I must have missed the memo. You aren't supposed to be checking in until 2 pm. Luckily there aren't any guests here. It would be an incredibly embarrassing situation, don't you think, if guests were still here when you arrived?'

They didn't bat an eyelid. 'Honey, we really want that washing powder, can you go get it now?'

As it turned out, the guests had a great stay. Had I said what I really wanted to say when they arrived hours early and without notice, then I am positive they would have complained to Airbnb and given me a bad review.

There are times as a host when you have to bite your tongue and remember the customer is always right. If you let guests know the lay of the land and give them a clear set of house rules, they will generally respect the guidelines and do the right thing.

Juls was a fabulous host who was warm and welcoming with attentive communication. Everything was clearly explained … The apartment is everything you need … The small touches that Juls adds are great …. Had a great stay. Thanks, Juls. Anita

Secret # 14: Set boundary lines and make things work for you

It's your business so operate it in a manner that works for you. Sometimes you will get guests who will make unreasonable demands or who will do unreasonable things. On occasion, you may have to bite your tongue and take a nuanced approach – your 5 star Superhost status may depend on it.

15

The Little Things

*Here is a simple but powerful rule: always give people
more than what they expect.*

Neslon Boswell

After almost two years of running my Airbnb, I left it in the
capable hands of Sharon and went on a trip to Boston. Whenever
I stay at an Airbnb, I observe what the host has done well and
what needs improvement. For example: Is the accommodation
clean? Has the host thought of my needs? What made my stay
special? The Boston Airbnb left a lot to be desired. This is what
I wrote after my stay:

How much toilet paper is there?
*There was only half a roll of toilet paper in the apartment. There wasn't
even a box of tissues to tide me over. Very disappointing!*

Is the accommodation clean?
*The apartment was clean, but there was no sheet or a doona cover on
the bed. Disturbing and unhygienic!*

Is there milk?

No milk upon arrival. Some people may have black tea or coffee, but I don't.

Are coffee and tea provided?
No coffee or tea. I am not impressed I had to go out in the pouring rain (and there was no umbrella) after a long flight to buy some coffee.

Is there anything that stands out?
No magazines or books. No decent TV. No pay TV. Nothing to make me smile.

Has the host thought of my needs?
Not at all. No sheet on the bed and the doona had no cover. Two flat, lumpy pillows that were horrible, and this in turn affected my sleep (I didn't have any), and I now have a very sore neck. There was a lamp with the cord running over the bed to the outlet on the opposite side. No bloody toilet paper. I wanted to leave after the first night.

Is the host responsive?
The host did reply to my queries in a timely fashion. Appreciated.

Was check-in simple and drama free?
Yes, check-in was pretty straightforward.

What made my stay special?
One of the most disappointing Airbnb stays I have experienced!

Meeting expectations

When I arrived in Boston, straight from a long-haul flight from Australia, I was met with one lonely cup and one lonely spoon.

That was it. That was the full extent of the supplies. I had to go and buy coffee, milk and toilet paper in the pouring rain – with no umbrella! It rains a lot in Boston and so I had to buy one of those as well. I mean, really? I had paid a small fortune for this experience, and the host had forgotten the most important aspect of Airbnb – the guest!

The host of this Airbnb provided me with a pretty awful experience, and you will not be surprised to know that he received a pretty average review. The apartment was in a good location which I gave credit for. But for the most part, I was blunt. After reading my review a person would, I think, have been reluctant to pay to stay there, even if it was at a reasonable rate. I pointed out its shortcomings because potential guests needed to know the truth. If I had seen an honest review before I had booked, I would not have stayed there. Was this avoidable? Absolutely! All the host had to do was put a bit of effort into his Airbnb, and I would have given him a fantastic review.

Make no mistake, people will remember the things that annoy them, even if in your eyes it seems minor. For me it's running out of toilet paper, which is why it is on the top of the list. As a host, I provide plenty of it. It is cheap to buy, and it can be very irritating for a guest if they have to go out and buy some because you did not provide enough, especially for a short stay.

Invest in the little things

On several occasions, I've stayed in accommodation where I ended up having to buy a frying pan because the one provided by the host was a hack. Every time I cooked, the food stuck to the pan and the meal was ruined. This was seriously annoying. I was on vacation, and I had to go out to buy a frying pan because the one on offer was useless.

I made sure I bought really good pots and pans when I set up my apartment. They are often on sale, so I didn't have to spend a fortune. I also put a blurb in my manual asking people to hand wash the pots and pans. After five years, they were still in great working order.

These may seem little things, but little things matter. They are the things people can get very annoyed about. They are the things people remember and put in their review. People are more likely to forgive you if they find there are no towels, than if there is no milk in the fridge for their coffee. Guests will often forgive a mistake (having no towels is obviously a mistake) which can be quickly corrected, but not a conscious decision by the host that seems penny-pinching (not providing milk or coffee, for example, is penny-pinching).

Little gestures make the guests feel the host has gone that extra mile for them.

The little things are really what make a wonderful and memorable experience. It's the little gestures from hosts that you remember the most. It is so exciting when you arrive somewhere and there is a bottle of wine or some chocolates waiting for you, or there is the smell of freshly ground coffee ready to be brewed. Those little gestures make the guests feel the host has gone that extra mile for them.

Juls couldn't have been more friendly, helpful and welcoming from the moment we booked to after we left the gorgeous apartment. Other reviewers have raved and so do we. Perfect location, beautifully equipped and stylish, not to mention cosy

and comfortable. Really appreciated the little thoughtful extras such as umbrella, first aid box (thankfully no need to use) and the stack of brand-new magazines. Thank you, Juls, for being the most lovely host and for making your apartment available.
Adele

We all want to feel special, right? So, although the big things (a good bed, soft towels, clean apartment) matter, if you want to be a Superhost, doing the big things is not enough – you need to offer that little bit more, you need to go above and beyond.

Oprah once said that validation is the most important thing we can give to each other, and it's free. It's as simple as letting people know, 'I see you. I hear you. And what you say matters.'

It is true for all of us. All we want to know is 'Did you hear me?' and 'Does what I say matter to you?' People want to feel special, to know someone cares about them. Each and every one of us wants to be heard somehow. We all want to be validated.

That is the secret to being a Superhost. You need to make your guests feel special, that they matter, that you hear what they want and will do your best to give them what they want.

I believe this is the magic I gave to my guests, and you can read that in their reviews. I gave my guests an 'experience'. I didn't just provide a bed and a shower for them, I made them feel special.

What do guests want?

When I was setting up my Airbnb, I prepared a 'What do I like?' list. I also looked at what Adam likes, as he has different wants and needs to me. I love it when the host provides good coffee when I stay at an Airbnb. I love a variety of teas. I love a good magazine to read. I love comfortable pillows and a comfortable mattress. I love soft towels. Adam loves chewing gum (go figure), fast wi-fi, a decent sized television and Netflix.

Fast wi-fi

Best thing about staying at Juls' apartment is Juls. Her communication was so friendly, prompt and thoughtful. Her little welcoming touches and attention to detail was outstanding. The apartment was styled beautifully, spacious for 2 people, comfortable, great appliances, fast reliable wi-fi and the location couldn't be better for access to local restaurants and cafes. Melbourne is a wonderful city, we walked everywhere from this central location. Would highly recommend staying with Juls. Thanks again, Juls. Mandy

These days, wi-fi is like food – everyone needs it, every day. I have stayed in many an Airbnb where there is no wi-fi or the wi-fi is limited (if you want extra you have to pay for it), and I have often ended up having to use my mobile data. One of the most common questions I was asked by potential guests was whether the apartment had wi-fi and if it was fast, and so I provided the best wi-fi I could. I recently stayed in a gorgeous apartment, but there was a crappy television and bad reception, and they only provided two gigabytes of free daily data. There was absolutely no generosity shown by the host.

Public transport cards

As I wanted to make life as easy as possible for my guests, I provided pre-paid cards to use on public transport. In Melbourne, the easiest way to get about town, other than on foot, is to catch public transport. To do this you need what's called a myki card. Using public transport without one means risking getting a hefty fine.

I would put ten dollars on the cards, and the guests would 'top' them up as necessary. Too easy! At the end of their stay, they would leave the cards for the next guests. Guests thought the cards were a very nice and very practical gesture as they didn't have to buy a card and throw it out when they left.

Juls has thought of everything to make your stay a memorable experience here. It really did exceed our expectations, and we will be back. We liked the extra little touches like the champagne and the MYKI cards and the little extras you may have forgotten to pack – even toothbrushes. We highly recommend. Sandra

Bottled water

Bottled water is a winner. As my apartment was in the beating heart of Melbourne, guests did a lot of sight-seeing. With a supply of bottled water in the fridge, all they had to do was grab as many bottles as they needed, and they were on their way.

This is a superb one-bedroom apartment ... well appointed with plenty of essential supplies. The cold bottled water was most welcomed after a hot day traveling. Quality fixtures and fittings (very comfortable bed) and surprisingly quiet considering you're in a busy lane ... Juls was quick to answer any messages and gave very detailed arrival instructions. I can highly recommend her and her beautiful apartment. Michelle

Pay television or streaming service

Providing a video streaming service, such as Netflix or Stan, is a sure-fire winner. It is much better to pay around twenty dollars a month to have the whole box and dice with Netflix or Stan and get an array of decent shows to watch, than to provide only free-to-air television or even Foxtel (Foxtel costs a bomb and you usually only get the Foxtel 'Basics' (for the price of a streaming service), which is pretty limited). Guests love having a streaming service. It is really nice for them to come back from a big day out sight-seeing and put their feet up with a drink and have some decent entertainment. It's even better if they get to watch the shows on a big screen.

Even if your guests don't watch any programs, a good quality television looks fantastic. I can't tell you how many times I have stayed at a gorgeous Airbnb and there has been a crappy little television in the corner of the room. It really brings down the tone of the place, and it looks like the host is not concerned with the comfort or needs of their guests. A large, high-quality (tax deductible) television is a great investment, and guests will rave about it.

The stay at Juls' place was nothing short of awesome. The place is exactly as it is on the listing and located conveniently within the CBD. Detailed instructions were also given to locate and access the apartment. There was also a number of thoughtful provisions, including a pair of myki cards for guests and a smart TV with Netflix. I would highly recommend Juls' place for anyone traveling to Melbourne! Jarrod

Magazines

Magazines are such a fabulous touch. I provided a variety of the latest magazines for both guys and gals. I am sure you have stayed in lots of places where the magazines are old or uninteresting. I mixed it up and offered what was 'in' and 'cool' at the time and, most importantly, I replaced the magazines each month. Old magazines always make me think of a waiting room at a doctor's surgery, where there are twenty boring, dog-eared magazines dating back to 2005. Get creative. You want hip, trendy and new! This was a big hit with my guests, and I got to enjoy the (tax deductible) magazines when I changed them over each month. Once I had read them, I gave them away – doctors and hairdressers always appreciate new magazines for their waiting room.

An amazing place! Juls' style can't be faulted, and often we found ourselves saying 'wow, this is really good quality'. Little things like quality tissues, little welcome chewing gum and Christmas chocolates, Bose audio, current (and stylish) magazines ... everything was done to perfection. Highly, HIGHLY recommended! John

Tea and coffee

I once stayed at an Airbnb where the host had a row of canisters with every imaginable variety of tea. Peppermint, chamomile, Irish breakfast, sencha, detox – you name it, there was a canister for each one. It looked great and added that extra something to the feel of the kitchen. Something so simple had a fantastic effect on me, so I took note of that and bought a few for my Airbnb. I didn't have a row of them because I didn't have the space, but a few cool cannisters was a nice touch. You don't need to spend up big. Go to Kmart or Big W and buy a couple of jars. Or, like me, you might want to go the extra mile and purchase some personalised canisters from https://lovetea.com.au/product-category/tea/ceramic-canisters/. It's the little things that make a big impression.

Although my apartment is surrounded by awesome cafés, and a lot of guests bought their coffee from those cafés, I still provided some coffee for them in the apartment as, again, it is a nice touch. My apartment had both a coffee machine and a coffee plunger, because guests don't always want to spend time using a machine. You don't need to do the same, but even if you provide one or two coffee options you will increase your likeability.

I have often stayed at accommodation where they don't provide any coffee, only the coffee machine or a plunger. What is the sense in that? It is such a small investment to provide a bag of ground coffee or coffee beans. You may not think that coffee is a big thing, but it is for some guests.

The apartment was just fantastic — and Juls would be the best host I've had — with special touches like champagne and chocolates! The apartment was so clean and well appointed — it smelled lovely and fresh — and included a Nespresso machine, kitchen basics like olive oil, a bath and a very large smart TV! The location is very handy for quick shopping expeditions — there are many restaurants in surrounding streets — and in particular the renowned Hardware Société is just downstairs for superb breakfasts or lunch. Highly recommended for the perfect Melbourne stay — for business or pleasure. Lynette

Some of the other things I made available for my guests were: umbrellas, travel adaptor, chargers, sunscreen, and ear plugs. There are so many little things you can provide that will win your guests over.

With longer stays – a week or more – or if I knew the guest was having a special occasion such as a birthday or an anniversary, I would provide a bottle of champagne or wine. While it is an additional cost for you, the host, when the guest is staying for a long period the cost of the wine in comparison to the price of the stay is small (and remember, the cost is tax deductible).

Juls even left us a bottle of bubbly to celebrate our anniversary! She is an exceptional host. If we ever return to Melbourne that's the only place we would stay. Thank you Juls for everything. Sharon

My guests have adored all the things I have spoken about here. Do yourself a favour, and don't scrimp on the small things. Invest in providing little things your guests will appreciate. Even one or two little extras will send the message to your guests that you are thinking of their needs.

Secret # 15: Be generous with your guests

It's easy to be generous with your guests – a small gift for a special occasion, a few extra things in the kitchen cupboard, a comfortable mattress, a little extra information. All these little things show you care, and your guests will respond to your generosity by writing rave reviews and returning again and again.

16

Let's Talk

The single biggest problem in communication is the illusion that it has taken place.

George Bernard Shaw

Communication comes naturally to me. My mother used to say, 'Juls, you were born with a phone in your hand' – and that was before mobile phones! I can talk the leg off a chair (ask anyone who knows me). My dad, God bless his soul, would constantly tell me to 'Stop asking questions'. At times I would even get, 'Will you shut up', because I never stopped asking questions as a child, and I just never stopped talking.

Guests love it when you reply straight away.

Communication is paramount if you want to be a successful Airbnb host. One of my biggest drawcards as an Airbnb host was my communication. Yes, I will happily give myself a huge pat on the back for these skills. What is the secret?

First and foremost, you need to respond quickly and think ahead. As soon as I received a booking request I responded to it as quickly as possible. I made sure requests came through to my mobile phone so I was able to reply to the booking without delay. Guests love it when you reply straight away. It gives a great first impression and first impressions count for a lot.

Once the booking was confirmed, I would send the guests a welcome message with a bucketload of information for their stay:

Hi Karen,

Thanks for your booking.

A little bit of information for your trip. You may know Melbourne well, but I like to give people as much info as I can.

There are several ways to get into town from the airport. When you arrive into Melbourne, you can either catch a cab, Uber or a great way to get into town is the SkyBus. It is very popular and very reasonable. It's a 20-minute bus ride from the airport into town and runs 24/7. There are signs everywhere at the airport where SkyBus is located so you can't miss it. There is a SkyBus free hotel transfer when you get to town. The shuttle drops guests off at various hotels. The closest hotel to the apartment is Adina Apartment Hotel in Queen Street and it's about a 6-minute walk to the apartment. You can jump on the SkyBus website and it has all the information you need about SkyBus and the free hotel transfer service. It's $19 one way and $38 return. SkyBus website: www.skybus.com.au

Here are a few good websites for things to do in Melbourne while you're here:

www.airbnb.com.au/things-to-do/melbourne

https://theculturetrip.com/pacific/australia/articles/21-awesome-free-things-to-do-in-melbourne/

https://theculturetrip.com/pacific/australia/articles/20-unmissable-attractions-in-melbourne/

The Victoria market is a winner. Southbank/casino strip is lots of fun. The Botanical gardens are lovely. The art gallery or the museum may tick your boxes. If you need help deciding on a particular thing you want to do or a restaurant you want to go to but aren't sure, let me know as I may be able to let you know if it's a winner or not.

A few well-regarded places to eat if you are looking for a restaurant:

Becco —www.becco.com.au

Syracuse — syracuserestaurant.com.au

Punch Lane — punchlane.com.au

Rosa's Canteen —www.rosascanteen.com.au

There is a fabulous bar next door to the apartment called La La Land. It's a great little spot to relax and have a vino and it's only a couple of steps from home:

www.lalaland.com.au/melbourne/

The trams within the city are free to travel on, which is fabulous. But if you're venturing out of the city or catching trains or buses you will need to use a myki card. I have some myki cards in the desk drawer at the apartment for you to use on your visit to get to the hospital and about town. It has information in the manual on how myki works. You can top up the myki cards at any train station, newsagent or 7/11. There is a 7/11 close by at 228 Queen Street or Melbourne Central station is about a 3-minute walk away. Myki website: www.ptv.vic.gov.au/tickets/myki

The apartment manual is in the desk drawer, and that goes through everything about the apartment: internet codes, TV and Netflix; how to use appliances; transport; supermarkets – everything you will need to know for your stay.

The apartment is between a restaurant called White Mojo and Hardware Street Cafe. The apartment is on Level 2. When you walk out of the lift it's just to the left – No. 8.

I will send the codes to get into the apartment 24 hours before you arrive (building and apartment are keyless). I will also send to your mobile some photos and a short video I put together on how to open the front door to the apartment.

Cheers,

Juls

☆

As you can see, I provided my guests with a lot of information. I did this because guests would often ask me a lot of questions and they tended to be the same questions. How do I get to your apartment from the airport? How will I collect the keys? What are some things I should do in Melbourne? Where is the nearest supermarket? What restaurants do you recommend? It was far better to provide that information in my welcome message than wait to be asked. Guests will absolutely love that you have taken the guesswork from them, and they will be stoked that you took the time to do this.

Before we even arrived in Australia, Juls was in contact with us to prep us for our arrival. She provided such great service. Seeing her stylish accommodation, enjoying her vibrant neighborhood, and eating at her recommended restaurants, made me wish even more we had booked a longer stay! Juls is a pro in the hospitality industry. Susan

Preparing your guests for their stay

The quick video I sent to guests before their arrival, on how to open the apartment door, turned out to be an absolute winner. The apartment was self-check-in; it was keyless and had an electronic keypad that required a code for entry. Some guests would get confused about how to use the electronic keypad, even though I sent detailed instructions on how to open the front door. On occasion I had to go to the apartment because a guest wasn't able to let themselves in. One day when I was at the apartment, I had an 'aha moment' and realised I could make a quick twenty-second video of how to open the front door. That way if a guest couldn't work it out, they would have a visual aid to help them. Let me tell you, that video hit the spot. People loved this gesture, and I didn't get any more texts or calls asking how to open the door.

Because guests don't tend to think about their upcoming stay until close to arrival time, I would send an email a week before they arrived just to say hello and let them know I would be in touch again twenty-four to forty-eight hours before they were due to arrive. At that time, I'd give them the codes to get in, photos of the building, the video of how to open the door to get into the apartment and anything else they needed to know.

It is very important to give guests the 'heads up' so they don't have to search for information or chase you up at the last minute. It shows you are efficient and gives the guest confidence that they have chosen a good place with an attentive host. Take the guesswork away, and make life easier for your guests.

We stayed at Jul's place for seven nights. It was beyond our expectation. It is a lovely, quiet and comfortable apartment in the best location. One of the rare Airbnb's that have all amenities one would need ... Juls answered any questions we had immediately, and her instructions covered anything you would need to know. We would consider her to be a super host. Truly. Larry

The other benefit of proactively providing lots of information up front is that your guests will not ask you so many questions. This makes it easier for you to run your Airbnb.

The apartment manual

As well as sending guests information ahead of their stay, I provided a comprehensive apartment manual. The manual provides the guests with information about the apartment: how to use appliances, what the wi-fi code is, where to shop, places to eat, transport, what's happening about town, and much more.

The first thing I do when I arrive at accommodation is look for the manual. I want to know all the ins and outs of the accommodation and how everything works. In most cases, I find a one-page sheet that doesn't really give much information. My bugbear has always been remotes. Often there are two or three remotes: one for the television, one for the pay TV or the DVD/ CD player, and a spare. I then have to spend time working out which is which and how everything works. Note to all those hosts out there: Not everyone knows how to work the remotes. Assume no-one gets it. I was adamant my apartment manual was going to be a one-stop shop. Guests would get the Rolls Royce of manuals – step-by-step instructions for everything.

Guests loved my apartment manual, and they appreciated that I had gone to the effort to produce a thorough and comprehensive booklet that provided an abundance of information (a copy of my apartment manual has been reproduced at the back of this book). Okay, I accept that some people don't give two hoots about a manual and have no interest in reading one (including my dearly beloved husband), but for most guests not having a comprehensive apartment manual can be a challenge. While my style of manual may not be everybody's cup of tea, I can assure you, many people have commented on how thorough and how easy to read it was, and how they appreciated the detailed instructions.

In my apartment manual, I even explained the easiest way to open the balcony door. There was a fine art to it as you had to slide the double glazing across to access the door, and the double glazing was fiddly. Explaining how to open the balcony door saved me having to get the double glazing repaired, which I had to do at times when it wasn't opened properly.

It won't cost you anything to put together a manual, just some time. So don't scrimp or cut corners. Go through every little thing in your Airbnb, especially where you need to push a button or put in a code, and put it in your manual. That way you will have thought of everything. Your guests will be able to go through the steps in the manual, and you won't have to take calls late at night because someone can't get the Netflix to work.

Juls was such a great host from communicating everything about the apartment even before I arrived to helping with all my little questions after I arrived. The apartment was clean,

bright and such a lovely place to stay in, it was tucked away in a little lane but yet walking distance to everything that makes Melbourne such a great city — the trams, the markets and malls and all the great food and coffee places were literally just a few minutes away. The apartment was a perfect home for my seven-night stay and would definitely love to be back!
Tiffany

I also had a folder in the apartment with all the appliance manuals. I referred the guests to the appliance manuals if they were unable to work out how to use a particular appliance. As well, there was our friend Google. And if all else failed, I was always available.

An apartment manual is an absolute godsend for both guests and hosts. I had so many guests thanking me for making their life easier by having such a great manual. I highly recommend putting in the initial work to get great results. Believe me, this is going to set you apart from the rest of the hosts out there.

Secret # 16: Communication is crucial to success

Every moment of contact and every piece of information you provide is saying to your guest, 'Your enjoyment is important to me.' Whether it's a warm and helpful phone call, an informative email or a comprehensive guest manual, it all contributes to your guest having a memorable and enjoyable stay and leaving a great review. And remember, where possible, reply to questions straight away.

17

Hiccups

Even in the most difficult situation there is always, somehow, a way to triumph.

Ralph Marston

Sometimes there will be hiccups. When a hiccup occurs, you need to deal with it immediately and ensure it does not adversely affect your guest's stay. If you act quickly, nine times out of ten your guests will forgive you.

> *From check-in to check-out, Juls was the perfect host. Always quick to respond and keen to accommodate, each interaction was a delight ... We can't recommend this apartment (and Juls) highly enough!* Olivia

After I hired my cleaner, Sharon, my routine was to check the apartment after she (or one of her employees) had cleaned, to ensure that everything was tip top before my guests arrived. No matter how good your cleaner is, mistakes happen.

Sharon cleaned the apartment herself for many years, and she was fantastic. As she employed more people over time, things occasionally went wrong. Although most of her staff were excellent, with a large team it is hard to keep the standard of work consistently first class.

I had times when the cleaner would forget the towels or leave the toilet uncleaned (and there is nothing more gross for a guest than arriving to find a dirty toilet or hairs in the bath). Because I went in after each clean, I was able to fix these hideous mishaps. Not all people have that luxury. I made it my job to do this because, believe you me, you are guaranteed to find nasty surprises.

Sometimes, though not often, I went to check the apartment after a clean only to find the apartment had not been cleaned at all. I would contact Sharon and ask her to send someone NOW because the clean had been missed. On a rare occasion, I had to clean it myself.

Placating your guests when mishaps occur

Even when you think you are all over everything, things can sometimes go awry. On one particular occasion, I went to the apartment in the morning and noticed there were no towels left for the guest who was arriving in the evening. I messaged Sharon to say the cleaners had forgotten to put fresh towels on the bed. She said, 'No problem, Juls. They are being washed and I will get someone to drop them off.' I was comfortable with that, and I went on my merry way. Normally, Miss Anal that I am, I would have messaged Sharon to check that the towels had been dropped off, but for some reason I didn't. For whatever reason, the towels weren't dropped off. They had slipped through the cracks.

I usually contact guests soon after they arrive, to make sure all is okay. In this instance, the guest, Paul, wasn't checking in until 10 pm, so I told him I would check in to see how he was going the next day. The next morning, before I sent a text to see how Paul was settling in, I get a message from him: 'Juls, where are the towels?'

I knew immediately the towels hadn't been placed back in the apartment. Damn! Normally there are spare towels in the cupboard, so I texted back: 'Aren't they on the bed? If not, have a look in the cupboard as there should be a couple in there.'

Paul's response? 'None anywhere. I had to use a hand towel and have had to go buy a towel.'

Damn, damn, damn! (Or something like that.) I immediately called Sharon, who apologised and said she would drop them off within the hour.

Tell the story

I called Paul and apologised, and I told him I was mortified at what had happened. I told him the story and assured him that Sharon was on her way to drop off the towels. Always tell people the story. They really appreciate it.

Paul was very upset, and rightly so as he had to dry himself with a hand towel. You can imagine my embarrassment. I had to think fast so I offered him payment for the towel (what he paid, plus a bit extra) and asked what else I could do for him. I could hear in his voice that he was happy he was going to be reimbursed with a bonus, and that I was making an effort to make up for this annoyance. We ended up having a great conversation, and Paul, being a fellow Airbnb host, shared his own war stories. We exchanged a few more texts, and once the towels had been delivered, he was one happy chappy.

As you can see, things do go belly up even when you, the

host, have done everything right. My saving grace was that I acted promptly, told Paul the story and made amends for the inconvenience he had experienced. He was a reasonable person, like most guests are, and so he understood the situation and I was able to ensure he enjoyed the rest of his stay at my apartment.

If possible, give your apartment the once over before your guests arrive. Understand that mistakes happen – towels are not left, coffee isn't replenished, dishes aren't cleaned, or the cleaner has gone to the toilet and has forgotten to flush it (yes, that has happened).

If I was going away or not able to check the apartment before a guest's arrival, I let them know. I would tell them Sharon was looking after the apartment, and if they had any concerns, she was the person to contact. If you notify your guests that you are unavailable during their stay, and if something does go wrong, chances are they will understand because you have explained it to them. Being up front really does make the world of difference.

If there were hiccups, like the air conditioner going on the blink or the dishwasher acting up, I would always offer to come in and look at the problem or call in a handyman to fix it. Often guests were happy to let it get sorted after their departure, but I made sure the guests knew I would do whatever was necessary to get the problem fixed. Guests are just happy that you care.

Communication is the key

Similarly, it's worthwhile notifying your guests if there is anything going on in your pad or in the neighbourhood that may affect their stay. Your guests will appreciate it. I was probably way over the top with letting my guests know of any changes or hiccups, but I thought that was better than not saying anything at all. It can really irritate a guest if they are greeted with a little surprise, whether it be building works next door or a broken door handle.

Weigh up what you think guests should know; it is always better to be upfront with what is happening than to say nothing as this can be your undoing. Mark my words, don't think you can get away with hiding information and not telling guests what is going on. They will find out and you will look like an idiot.

And if a guest asks questions and you have absolutely no idea what the answers are? No problem. I never told my guests, 'Sorry, I have no idea and can't help you.' I would always try to give them something, or guide them to a place that would be able to help them. That was often simply sending them a link to a website that could assist them. The main thing is to show that you have tried.

Secret # 17: Take immediate action and tell the story

When a guest contacts you about a problem, it's time to go into rapid response mode. Saying you'll look into it when they leave, or when you've got time, may not be good enough. Find out what the issue is, let the guest know you'll do something about it, keep in touch and get the problem solved as quickly as possible. And when things go awry, tell the story, most guests will forgive you and understand.

18

Handle with Care

A cynic is a man who knows the price of everything and the value of nothing.

Oscar Wilde

Towards the end of 2016, with our sixteen-day Everest Base Camp trek looming, we went on a 'training run' to the Grampians. It was a warm day, and I do not do well in the heat (I think it's because I have low blood pressure). We got about halfway up, going along at Adam's brisk pace, and I felt faint. We had to stop while I rested. Adam and the kids thought I would really struggle in the Himalayas. I was worried myself, terrified in fact, but, come hell or high water, we were going to do this trek.

When the trip came around, it was brutal. There were fourteen of us, most in their early twenties. For ten days we climbed to Everest Base Camp, 5364 metres above sea level – in winter! (In fact, Everest Base Camp is that same height above sea level in summer too, but you know what I mean.) Our coldest night was minus twenty-six degrees Celsius, with no heating. We trekked between five and eight hours a day through difficult circumstances. There were bouts of gastro, pounding headaches brought on by altitude sickness and the extreme cold.

I remember one young guy, in his early twenties, was curled up in a foetal position crying because it was all too much for him.

Adam and Paris both got sick. Paris was the worst, throwing up and unable to keep food in her stomach; but she kept going and did not complain. Fortunately, I did not get sick on the trek (though I did bring back a gastrointestinal infection that manifested itself back in Australia), and I had no trouble making it to Everest Base Camp.

I wasn't the fastest or the most elegant of the group, but I became an inspiration to my family, and it felt like they were seeing me for the first time – not a weak link after all, but a warrior with an indomitable spirit.

Our guide, who had been trekking for fourteen years, said Alec and Paris were the bravest kids he had ever encountered on the trek. They never whinged or complained, they just got on with it. What they learnt on the mountain they will carry with them through their life. What a gift I was able to give to them.

After his cancer operations, Adam had changed his lifestyle and was in pretty good shape, so the climb didn't challenge him from a fitness perspective. What I found surprising was, he missed the comforts of home. He had it in his mind that when we stopped at the waystations each night, we would go inside, take our gear off and relax in the warmth with some food and wine in front of the fire. In actual fact, it was almost as cold inside as it was outside. On arrival at the inn, after a hard day's hiking, innkeepers would put yak dung in a tiny iron stove in the middle of the room and light it. It would take half an hour to warm up slightly (I use the words 'warm up' very loosely) and the fifteen of us would huddle around it trying to get warm.

Needless to say, we would turn in very early. Nevertheless, Adam really relished the fact that we, as a family, were experiencing such harsh conditions and were getting through it, and he was blown away by the local people and the way they lived.

For me, the trek was the achievement of a lifetime and it helped contribute to my self-belief, which was a huge benefit in helping me better manage my Airbnb and my guests. Most of my guests were delightful and gave me great joy, but there were a few who required careful handling, such as 'demanding divas' and 'bargain basements'.

The demanding divas

'Demanding divas' was my pet name for those guests who thought I was their travel agent or their personal assistant. Don't get me wrong, I was always happy to help a guest, as that is one of the roles of a host, but some guests would continuously message me and others were so over the top with their requests, I would scratch my head in amazement.

My advice is to get on the front foot immediately. It is important to help your guests, so always do some research, but don't spend hours and hours doing all the work for them. You want to be helpful, but you also want guests to think for themselves – 'Have you tried Google?'

Here are some of the more interesting questions I had over the years:

- *Where do we sit at Laver Stadium [for the tennis] so that we are not in the sun during the day? Should we get the tix plus dining now to be sure of good seats or wait to October and see which seats are still available (we'd love to be close to center court in Row B and it's now available)?*

- *I love my coffee. What kind of coffee maker do you have – plunger or coffee machine. Do you have salt, sugar, pepper? What are your kitchen supplies and what do you have in your pantry?*
- *What size is the bath – is it shallow or deep as I love a deep bath. How big is it?*
- *What's the bed like – soft or hard as I can only sleep on a soft mattress. What is the comfort level?*
- *I need to buy floaties now! Where do I go now to buy?* [This demand came through at eleven o'clock at night!]

I have learnt through experience that it is best not to engage in longwinded conversations with people who ask questions such as these. With the guest who had questions about the tennis, I sent a link to the Tennis Australia website. I kept my response short and to the point. If I had gone into detail about the tennis, I suspect I would have been in for a long, drawn-out match, going back and forth until a tie break in the fifth set. Keep it simple.

The 'bargain basements'

Other guests that need careful handling are those who ask for a discount.

In response to requests I considered ridiculous, I politely said, 'Thanks but no thanks,' and sent them on their way. But the odd person slipped through the cracks, caught me in a 'generous' mood or booked my place months and months in advance (at prices which I had not updated to reflect periods of high demand) and I couldn't do a thing about it.

I also occasionally gave a discount to repeat guests, even if they did not ask for one. But mostly, if I was asked for a discount I would respectfully decline. I had an automatic seven-day (fifteen per cent) and one-month (twenty-five per cent) discount as part of my listing on the Airbnb website, and I did not need to provide any further discounts because I was generally booked out.

We have all come across hagglers in one situation or another. I once had a bread maker for sale on eBay for $10. One person who wanted to buy the bread maker tried to bargain on it. I couldn't believe it. The bread maker cost hundreds of dollars back in the day, and it was still in mint condition. This person kept going back and forth about the price. She even brought up the fact that she would have to get transport from somewhere an hour away to collect the bread maker. I roared with laughter. She was haggling over spending $10 for a bread maker, and her fare on transport would cost more than that. You can't make this stuff up!

One person contacted me and wanted to stay at my apartment for three months but could only afford a couple of hundred dollars a week. I have had other people say they want to stay for two weeks and, 'What is the best deal ya can do me?' And because of my apartment's location, I frequently got enquiries from university students. They usually wanted to stay for six months but wanted to do a deal. I had offers of $500 a week for six months' accommodation. As appealing as that is for a lot of people, for me it would have meant losing money. I didn't need to do deals. My apartment was a top performer and was near to full capacity, so I was not in need of long-term stays at low prices. The apartment brought in upwards of $5k in an average month and upwards of $6k in a great month, so $500 per week wasn't going to cut the mustard I'm afraid.

If someone wants to book a lengthy stay and pay the going rate, you can show generosity and offer your guests a discount or some other incentive. If I got a really lucrative booking, I provided the cleaning for free for the duration of their stay. Offering a clean is a win–win. The guest is ecstatic because they are getting a cleaner; you are guaranteed your Airbnb is going to remain clean; and your cleaner can keep an eye on how things are being looked after.

With guests who want to barter, bargain, or negotiate, my advice is to put a stop to it immediately! Potential guests are of course entitled to contact you so as to ask for a discounted rate. However, they can become a bottomless pit of time wasting and will possibly drive you demented with their demands. If you start a dialogue with a bargain hunter who wants to negotiate a lower rate for your Airbnb, then believe me, they will be a ball and chain around your neck. I have had first-hand experience with these people, and if you get involved with them it can very quickly turn into a nightmare.

Tweaking your website listing

One way to avoid hagglers is with the Airbnb bookings system. Airbnb gives you two options in relation to how you accept guest bookings. You can allow *instant booking*, whereby if the guest meets all of Airbnb's requirements, they automatically book your Airbnb on request, no questions asked. Alternatively, you can vet your enquiries via the *reservation request* channel, in which case the guest contacts you directly about booking your Airbnb and you have the option to accept or decline the guest's request to book.

For some time I vetted my guests and preferred them to come through the reservation request channel. That way I could gauge who they were, get an idea of their Airbnb credentials and history, and see if they were going to be the right 'fit' for my apartment.

As time went on, I decided to go down the instant booking route. With instant booking, guests can book without having to send a request to you. So long as they meet the Airbnb criteria, they are instantly approved and booked by the website. Airbnb encourages hosts to allow instant bookings, and guests generally like the convenience of being able to book without having to interact with the host.

An instant booking may seem like the easier option, but it does bring its own headaches, as I experienced with guests who didn't suit my apartment and who caused me a lot of drama. On many occasions it was because they expected lots of hand holding and for me to meet them on arrival. I didn't do either. But with instant bookings I had no opportunity to weed out those people.

I ended up going back to reservation request as the booking method so that I could vet every guest who wanted to stay at my apartment. That way I had more control. You can always do what I did and try both. You will soon get a vibe for what works best for you. Just know that the quick way is not always the best way! And even with reservation requests, I occasionally got a 'bargain basement' guest who fell through the cracks. One such guest was a lady called Sandra. She wanted to stay for six nights and contacted me to ask the best price I could offer. My instinct told me not to engage, to just say the price is the price, but for some reason I thought I would give her the seven-night discount (15% off the daily rate). Even as I hit the reply button, I regretted it – it was against what my gut was telling me to do.

You can always tell a little bit about the guest by their initial message. Because Sandra had asked for the 'best total price' for her stay, I knew she was a bargain hunter and was haggling to get the best deal. I didn't need to entertain the idea of a discount, but I went against my better judgment and for that I paid the price.

You may be wondering what my problem was in giving Sandra the discount for six nights that usually applied to seven nights. Well, because I provided so many essentials for my guests (basically they want for nothing), the price I charge is fair for the accommodation and the experience. As soon as I said to Sandra I would give her the discount, she pounced. She said she was deciding between my place and another. She told me all the things she loved: 'I love coffee. Do you provide coffee and essentials in the cupboard? Is the bath full size? How do I get to your place after I get off the SkyBus? Can you meet me at the apartment to check me in? Is the apartment close to trams?' And she hadn't yet booked her flights. Geez!

I knew it was a big mistake allowing this guest to stay, and I was racking my brain trying to work out how I could pull the pin. Technically you can't pull the pin and cancel a booking without a valid reason, so I needed a diplomatic way of backing out. I knew this guest required hand-holding, and I was not able to give that to her. My apartment catered to people who were self-sufficient, as it stated in my advertisement. I created my apartment for people who were independent and didn't need physical assistance during their stay. I let her know I was worried she would need someone who was on hand to meet and greet her, and I said I wasn't sure if my place was right for her. I tried, subtly, to get her to cancel.

She wasn't having any of it. She wanted to keep her reservation. I personally did not believe my apartment was the best choice for her, but I had to resign myself to the fact that she wanted to stay. Damn!

I knew from her barrage of questions she was going to be needy, and my instincts were right. As soon as she arrived she started messaging me.

The door is confusing.
There is a beeping sound coming from the lift.
WHAT IS IT? WHAT DO I DO?

I did a lot of deep breathing that week. Truth be told, I should have said *no deal*. I knew from the outset she was high maintenance, but I ignored my instincts, gave her a discount and I paid the price for securing a booking. Was it worth it? No! But I learned a valuable lesson. Trust your instincts with bargain hunters. Use your judgment, and if a potential booking doesn't feel right, then decline. That gut feeling will mostly be right.

One bargain hunter who slipped through the cracks on instant booking was Danny. He was coming to Melbourne for the Formula One Grand Prix, which was going to be held in March – eighteen months away! The first thing that popped into my mind when I saw the booking was, Oh shit, I forgot to put my rate up for that weekend. Now you must realise, if you own an apartment in Melbourne CBD, on a long weekend or a public holiday you can up your rate considerably. I could charge up to $400 a night on some public holidays (New Year's Eve, for example) and also an increased rate for the Grand Prix. It is a matter of supply and demand, and I had no problem in increasing my prices when demand was high. It is not price gouging; it is an outcome of a properly functioning market for services. When demand is high, prices go up.

I usually go through the calendar on the Airbnb website and make sure the rates are set for the coming year. Unfortunately, on this occasion, I had forgotten to go far enough in advance in my diary and on the Airbnb calendar, so Danny hit the jackpot. He not only got the weekly discount, he was also coming from the United States so the exchange rate was definitely in his favour. What a bargain! Unfortunately, he was also hard work. His manner was very gruff, and in our first interaction he went on about the nightly rate he was charged and how it was calculated. I explained that he was in the USA and I was in Australia, so he would need to take the exchange rate into account. I ended up, after much toing and froing, directing him to connect with Airbnb as to the intricacies of the booking (and exchange rates), because he was just not getting it.

He then came back with more questions. Is the mattress soft or firm? Do I have electric outlet adaptors? Could he and his wife drop their luggage off prior to check-in as they were arriving early? I was exhausted, and he hadn't even arrived yet. I felt impending doom. He was going to be a complainer. The punters who book far in advance and snap up a bargain can be serial pests. It's not enough that they are getting a fabulous deal, they continue to nit-pick about everything.

I was used to people asking me a mountain of questions, but he took it to a whole new level. I got a barrage of messages to say he was perturbed because the washing machine rim was dirty and the overhead fan in the bathroom ceiling was dusty. He explained that he had tried to clean the overhead ceiling fan in the bathroom with my vacuum cleaner, but it kept jamming. Anyway, he wanted me to come in and see him.

What annoyed me more than anything was the fact he took it upon himself to do housekeeping and maintenance. For starters, you have to take the overhead fan apart (usually accessed by a ladder) and clean it with a cloth. Also, my vacuum cleaner is an upright vacuum cleaner. It is very heavy and not to be used for lifting up above your head and cleaning ceiling fans. (The vacuum cleaner was never the same after he used it.) But most importantly, he must have been on a chair as I have very high ceilings, and he could have fallen off and done some serious damage to himself.

I was really annoyed, but I knew I had to stay calm. I told him not to do anymore home maintenance work and laid out the reasons why. I have no doubt he would have tried to sue me if he had hurt himself, and I was not going to take responsibility for his stupidity.

Bargain hunters can be down-right annoying as they expect the world and nit-pick about inconsequential things. Danny did not see what was right in front of him: all the positive, wonderful things about the apartment – its location, the surrounds, the array of goodies I had provided for him on arrival and the bargain price he paid for beautiful accommodation. He didn't appreciate the 'experience'. People like him are guests you don't need, as they are just never satisfied.

Some guests might not be a good fit

Occasionally you will get an enquiry where you know the guests aren't going to be the right fit for your Airbnb. How do you tell that person your Airbnb won't suit them without being offensive? If I felt my apartment wasn't a good fit for a potential guest, I'd let them know and give them the option to book somewhere else. I preferred to be honest rather than just accept anyone for the sake of a booking, and I didn't want the headache of that person complaining if they were not happy.

I had one couple who were very keen to stay, but I knew my apartment wouldn't suit their needs. The husband had a bad knee and he really struggled with stairs of any description. There is a step in my apartment between the bathroom and the living room, which for most people is fine but it is a step up and if you forget you could fall over (I have never had anyone fall, but there is always a first time.) They were an elderly couple, and they were keen for me to meet them on arrival. I could tell from the enquiry that they would be much better suited to a hotel or accommodation where there was a concierge. I wasn't going to be around to meet them or be available to help them on their trip, so I was honest and suggested a few other places I thought might be a better fit for them. They were very appreciative of my honesty and did decide to stay somewhere else.

Sometimes people still want to stay at your Airbnb, even if you suggest that it may be better for them to stay somewhere else. No problem. I was always honest, so there were no surprises for the guests when they arrived. Plus, I was covering myself. If the guests arrived and were unhappy with something and messaged me, I could say I provided them with all the relevant information to enable them to make an informed decision. It's not that I didn't want the business. It was because I could tell from the enquiry that my apartment may not have suited their needs. Mostly guests still wanted to book, but they were always very grateful I had been upfront and honest.

When you show the guest that you actually care, it will stay with them when they write a review.

Secret # 18: Operate your Airbnb in a manner that suits you

Be clear in your mind as to the type of guest you want to come and stay at your Airbnb. While it is important to get lots of bookings, not every guest is necessarily the right guest for you. Understand and actively engage with the Airbnb website so that the settings (instant book vs request; nightly rate; minimum stay, etc) suit you. Operating an Airbnb business can be fun and rewarding especially if you operate it in a way that works for you.

19

The Comforts of Home

The Noblest Art is that of making others happy.

P.T. Barnum

Some months after returning from our trek to Everest Base Camp, I received the following email from Airbnb:

> *Hi Juls,*
> *We're piloting a new program to showcase some of the best, highest quality homes in Melbourne and … yours stood out to us. So, I'm writing to let you know that [this listing has] been preselected for a special pilot: Best location in town!*

This pilot program became Airbnb Select. After agreeing to be part of the pilot program (what an honour!), I received another email from Airbnb:

> *Hi there Juls,*
> *… I know you are already in the process of making your beautiful home a part of Select and we are so excited!*
> *As part of our effort to launch Select to all guests and get them excited too, we need to produce a very special photo*

shoot at one or two of the very best Select listings within each market. We're looking for the most appealing and inviting spaces, which clearly reflect the care of their hosts. The purpose of these images is to represent the value of Select to all of our guests, and to headline each market.

I'm writing to you because we love your beautiful home, and if you are interested and timing works out with our production plan we would like to photograph it!

The Select program was re-branded as Airbnb Plus, and I was invited to be part of it. Whereas the Superhost status is a recognition of the host for their exceptional hospitality, the Airbnb Plus program recognises both the host and the outstanding quality, comfort and style of the property. Airbnb were recognising all the hard work I had put into buying the right property, styling it and maintaining it. I was thrilled.

All I can say is WOW! The moment we stepped through the door we could tell plenty of thought went into the look and feel of the whole gorgeous apartment. The interior design, quality finishes and tiny personal touches are what set off the vibe of this perfectly located, Luxury Home away from Home. The only regret we had was not booking a longer stay! We will definitely be staying back here the next time we are in town :) ... Thanks very much for the best first Airbnb experience! Angel

By 'property', the people at Airbnb aren't just talking about the building itself, they include all the things that go into making it comfortable and stylish.

Heating and air conditioning

One time, when I went on holiday, I stayed in a gorgeous little cabin in a delightful seaside town. The hosts were lovely and everything was just fabulous. They got a big, fat five-star review. I loved this cabin and had such a good time, I decided to go back in the winter months as staying by the sea in winter can be wonderful. I arrived cold and tired but excited at the thought of settling in with a hot cup of tea, my book and some warmth.

My stay didn't go quite as planned, because the heating was useless. There was a split system air conditioner, which would have been fine except the cabin had floor to ceiling windows. It was the middle of winter and it was very frosty outside. I had that split system unit going full pelt and it didn't make a lick of difference. It was absolutely freezing!

I hadn't given a second thought to the heating when I stayed in summer, because heating wasn't on my mind. Now the heating was very much on my mind. I spent a few days either wrapped up in blankets or in bed under the doona, and I ended up leaving early because I couldn't take being so cold and uncomfortable.

I never went back to the cabin again in winter, which is a damn shame as it is a wonderful place. If the cabin was warm and cosy, it would be lovely in winter. All the hosts needed to do was put some thought into how to keep the place warm, such as installing thick drapes on the windows to retain the heat, and I have no doubt it would be booked all year round.

I wanted to give my guests all the comforts of home, so I had an effective heating and cooling system. Most systems these days come with a timer or an app that you can set from your phone, so you can have your Airbnb at a nice, comfortable temperature when your guests arrive. It will make a wonderful start to their stay. Good heating and effective airconditioning are two 'must-haves' for a Superhost.

A good night's sleep

I also made sure I provided a comfortable mattress, quality pillows, luxurious linen and soft, fluffy towels.

Making sure your guests get a great night's sleep and have soft towels to dry themselves with after their shower will set you apart from the rest of the pack. While it may cost you time and money to get the right mattress and cost you a little extra for high quality linen and towels, it will be money and time well spent, and your guests will reward you in spades in the currency that matters – their reviews.

> *This unit had everything I needed ... [It] is well maintained and the bed [was] exceptionally comfortable ... I would definitely stay here again.* Sara

When I was setting up the apartment, it took me a while to find the right mattress. I did a lot of research, and I visited quite a few bed shops. What a nightmare! There is not a 'one size fits all' mattress, but a variety of mattresses each designed to suit a different requirement. Some people like a firm mattress while others like a soft one. I was looking for a mattress that was not too soft or too hard. I needed to please as many guests as possible.

The reason I was determined to get a decent mattress was because I had gone to hell and back when looking for one for my own bed. Finding a mattress that suited both Adam and me was a mission and a half, and we went through quite a few mattresses before we settled on 'the one'.

Adam gets very hot in bed and I don't, so we needed a mattress that wouldn't turn into a furnace as the heat built up during the night but that would feel warm enough for me. One salesperson convinced us that a particular mattress had been tested by NASA and that it would suit Adam's 'too hot' issue down to the ground. It didn't! We had to return the bloody thing.

If your guests don't sleep well, they won't be happy when they write your review.

I was then given a great tip from a lovely, knowledgeable mattress salesperson. She said the trick is to lie on the mattress for about twenty minutes. After that time, the mattress would start to become too hot or would be just right.

Despite this helpful advice, we still couldn't find a mattress that didn't end up making Adam feel very hot. We ended up having one made from scratch. It has been a marriage-saver.

You don't need to spend a fortune on getting a mattress custom-made, but I really do advise taking some time to buy a mattress that feels comfortable – not too hard and not too soft, somewhere in the middle is best.

For the apartment, I went to a reputable distributor and ended up buying something called a 'Spinal Care Plush Queen' and an upholstered base – by far the best mattress on the market at mid-range price. I wasn't going to spend a fortune on a bed for Airbnb, but I wanted a mattress that was 'just right' in comfort level for my guests. I obviously made the right choice because I have had quite a few guests ask me where I bought my mattress as they wanted to buy the exact same one.

If you want to be a Superhost, you need to take the time and effort to get a good mattress. If your guests don't sleep well, they won't be happy when they write your review.

Juls seriously has a gem with this apartment! Everything you need and more. Beautifully furnished and such a comfy bed. So comfy, we are buying one the same. We had such a lovely weekend. Thanks, Juls. Ben

From the mattress, I built upon the bedding, which is crucial to create a lovely 'experience' for the guests: great mattress, soft sheets, luscious doona, delicious pillows – it sounds like a meal.

Sheets, towels, and pillows

I again researched the best quality to give a fabulous night's sleep for my guests. There is nothing more wonderful after a long day of trekking about town, than slipping between luxurious sheets and laying your head on a comfortable pillow. Pima cotton above 500 thread count is a winner for linen. I bought a couple of good sets, and that is all you need as they will last a very long time.

But I didn't stop there. I wanted my guests to step out of the shower and dry themselves with a lovely, soft towel – to get that 'Aah' feeling. So, I made sure I invested in towels that were going to retain their softness, even after being washed multiple times.

If a guest does not sleep well because they are too cold or too hot, because the bed sags in the middle or squeaks when they roll over, or because the pillows are like pancakes, then it is unlikely they will give you a five-star review. Instead, they will be tired and grumpy, and with a tired and grumpy guest you will be lucky to get even a three-star review.

Guests may not always compliment you because they had a good night's sleep (although they often do), but they will certainly let you know if they were too cold, the pillows were lousy, or they were kept awake because of an inferior mattress.

These items are an investment in your business, so buy great quality from the start. Take pride in what you do, and strive to be the best host you can be. Mark my words, this will result in an outstanding review, each and every time.

This is the place to stay if you want comfort and style at a top location in the middle of Melbourne CBD. Super clean, stylish, incredible clever use of space so the apartment feels spacious, great kitchen amenities, great bathroom and very comfortable bed … We felt very welcome and looked after. Marjan

Secret # 19: Create a haven of comfort

The three pillars of comfort are: (i) a good night's sleep; (ii) a good hot shower with quality towels; and (iii) effective heating and cooling. If you have those pillars in place, your guests will come back for more. If any are missing, you'll have grumpy guests, rotten reviews and your bookings will dry up.

20

COVID-19 Comes Knocking

The truth is you don't know what is going to happen tomorrow. Life is a crazy ride, and nothing is guaranteed.

Eminem

When COVID-19 hit, life as we all knew it disintegrated before our eyes. For many hosts, business went from being fully booked to completely vacant. People were cancelling accommodation left, right and centre, bookings were plummeting, and travel had come to a standstill. In my case, because Melbourne was in lockdown, bookings crashed and burned.

As it turns out, this particular aspect of the pandemic was a blessing in disguise for me. How so, you ask? I had recently experienced a few disappointing encounters with one of my guests and with Airbnb customer service. The guest had complained about a moth in the bedroom, and that morphed into a broader (and false) complaint about the lack of cleanliness in my apartment, but that's a story for another day. When COVID arrived, Airbnb offered to reimburse hosts 25 per cent of their upcoming lost reservations. Airbnb also organised a Superhost Relief Fund to help people like me with their loss of bookings. I certainly had suffered a complete collapse in bookings – from 80–90 per cent fully booked to no bookings at all when COVID hit, all in the blink of an eye. Unfortunately, I didn't qualify for either of these financial assistance packages, which didn't make a lot of sense to me as I thought I ticked all the boxes and properly qualified for assistance. Airbnb said, '*No, sorry, we cannot help you.*' This experience opened my eyes to the fact that you aren't always going to get the support you think you need, or perhaps the support you deserve.

So what do you do when you are staring into the face of adversity?

One of my favourite quotes from Ryan Holiday's fantastic book, *The Obstacle is the Way,* is: 'The obstacle in the path becomes the path. Never forget, within every obstacle is an opportunity to improve our condition.'

Airbnb, like every organistaion and every individual, was dealing with the extraordinary circumstances of a pandemic. I understood this but also felt let down and a little sad that in my time of need, it didn't provide me with any financial assistance despite my years of hard work and my support of the company and its brand. Nevertheless, I decided to '*put my big girl pants on*' and find a way forward. As luck would have it, a new opportunity came knocking in the form of a phone call from my old pal, John Fuller, the agent who had sold me my Hardware Street apartment.

The property market was red hot in Melbourne just before the pandemic hit, especially for apartments. John planted the seed in my mind that it was a great time to sell and that he had prospective buyers ready. He had recently sold some apartments in the centre of the city that were comparable to mine for a tidy profit, and felt he could achieve a similar result for me.

Money talks. On the one hand I was torn because I loved my apartment, but the opportunity to sell was very tempting. As I was pondering the idea, COVID hit and all of a sudden the short-to-medium term viability of my Airbnb apartment was unclear. It was early days in the pandemic and we really didn't know what the effects of COVID were going to be. This uncertainty made selling the apartment an attractive prospect. It did feel like the stars were aligning.

By this time I had already ticked a lot of the boxes I had set out to achieve with my Airbnb, namely:

- *I was a successful Airbnb Superhost.*
- *I had owned the apartment for a number of years and I had operated a financially successful Airbnb business.*
- *I'd had fabulous experiences with my guests and had helped them to enjoy Melbourne.*

Combine all of the above with my recent experiences with Airbnb, which were less than perfect, plus the impact of the pandemic, and I started to think that perhaps this was a golden opportunity to sell.

Overwhelmingly, my Airbnb experience – despite the few hiccups I've written about here – was incredibly positive. The secrets I have shared in this book will help you to be a better host – even, perhaps, become a Superhost. Now I will add one more secret to the list, not to discourage you from embarking on your Airbnb journey, but to make sure you set off with your eyes wide open. The secret below is as true about Airbnb as it is about life.

Secret # 20: It's not all a bed of roses

Despite your best efforts, things don't always go the way you want. You're dealing with people, property, and a massive organisation. It's best to start your Airbnb journey knowing you will hit some bumps in the road, like you would any time you turn your hand to a business venture. However, being a Superhost is a rewarding experience and very achievable, provided you look after your guests along the way.

21

Time to Say Goodbye

Per ardua ad astra

Through hardship to the stars

What transpired next is what I call fate. John Fuller got in touch and told me that he had an offer from a potential purchaser to buy my apartment. John had periodically contacted me over the years, and I would always say, 'thanks but no thanks', as my Airbnb was thriving. I was committed to being an Airbnb host and I loved hosting. But this time was different. I had recently purchased an investment property and was about to embark on my first 'owner-builder' project. And, of course, COVID-19 was upon us, which had drastically changed the Airbnb landscape. The time was right to sell.

Even though I agreed to sell my apartment and my Airbnb journey as a host came to an organic end, I would not hesitate to jump back in and become an Airbnb host again should my circumstances change. Being an Airbnb host was one of the most satisfying experiences I have ever had, and I am very grateful to Airbnb (and, more importantly, to all my guests) for that opportunity.

My life has changed immeasurably since I started my

Airbnb journey and I have learned so much about running a business and people in general. Life is funny like that. A door opens and you don't know what is on the other side. But there is something inside of you that calls to you to take a 'leap of faith' and enter. Being an Airbnb host was the furthest thing on my mind when Adam first suggested it, and I did everything in my power to resist. But there was something within me that kept calling, until I couldn't resist any longer.

Becoming an Airbnb host and writing this book have been among the most incredibly challenging, and difficult, experiences I have ever had. Both experiences have given rise to much internal resistance on my part, debilitating fear, and terror. Many a night I would wake up and think, I can't do this. It's been an extraordinary, emotional roller coaster, but would I change a thing? Absolutely not.

By becoming an Airbnb host, I *found* myself. I unlocked untapped potential – potential I would never have explored or known I had if I hadn't leaped through that door into the unknown world of Airbnb. I became a pretty damn great Airbnb host and now I've written a book. Who knew I was capable of doing those things when I first ventured into Airbnb? Certainly not me.

My purpose in writing this book is to share my personal experiences as an Airbnb host with you and let you in on the secrets of my success. I have given you an inside look into what a host's life is like, and shared both the joys and the pitfalls that come with it.

My hope is that I have given you some tools so that you can become the Superhost I know you can be. Don't listen to the doubters and sceptics who say you can't do this. You can.

All you need is a smattering of faith, a dash of courage and a whole lot of grit and determination. Back yourself and go for it. Trust me, I'm a Superhost!

Happy Airbnbing!

Superhost Checklists

Checklist 1: Choosing your apartment to rent out on Airbnb

1. **Build a great team around you:** Accountant, lawyer or conveyancer, mortgage broker. You need people working for you who have the expertise to allow you to achieve what you want to achieve.

2. **Set up a company to own your property:** Putting your property into a company name as opposed to your individual name may provide you with asset protection.

3. **Location:** Will your guests want to stay in the area? Consider:
   - public transport (within easy walking distance)
   - village/village within the city – supermarket, shops, and restaurants close by
   - entertainment (beach, cinema, CBD)
   - major attractions
   - a nearby hospital or university (doctors, visitors, people taking courses all need accommodation).

4. **Size:** Consider a one-bedroom (maximum two-bedroom) apartment. Most guests are one person travelling alone, or a couple, so one bedroom will be sufficient most of the time to maximise booking rates. Also, one-bedroom apartments are cheaper, preserving your capital.

5. **Avoid new high-rise apartment buildings:** New high-rise apartments are built all the time. Your new apartment will be the newest and best only until the next newest

apartment is built. Highrise apartments do not, generally, have the same capital growth as those from smaller boutique apartment buildings.

6. **Choose a boutique apartment block, with a small number of apartments:** (8-12 if possible), and which has a point of difference to maximise capital growth in the longer term. For me, the point of difference was focusing on Art Deco apartments or those with period features. These types of features are sought after by buyers and, while you may pay a little more upfront, you will be rewarded by more capital growth in the long term. One reason they have better capital growth is because of the scarcity factor: Art Deco apartments are no longer (generally) being built; new high-rise buildings are mostly a dime a dozen.

7. **Layout:** Do not buy a property that has a higgledy-piggledy layout, one with secret doorways going off here, there and everywhere. If it is a strange set up, steer clear. Properties like this are confusing. People don't like to be confused. Keep it simple and go for appealing and functional designs.

8. **Noise:** Guests want peace and serenity. One of the top complaints from guests staying at Airbnbs is 'It's too noisy' or 'Loved the place but it's noisy'. People are very affected by noise so I would look very closely at the surrounds of the property you want to buy. Is it in a quiet street? If it's in a busy street, is it quieter at night? Hang out in the street to properly gauge the comings and goings, especially during the evening and at night-time. My apartment was (mostly) very quiet at night, but it still had double glazing because there was a bar a few doors away and it was located in the

city. If you love the property and it is in a busy spot, invest in double glazing.

9. **Entry:** Keyless entry is perfect for running an Airbnb, as you don't need to meet the guests; they can self check-in. If your apartment complex has a card for entry, it is a bit more complicated because you have to give the card to the guest. If the property has keyed entry, you need to be able to easily install a key safe/lockbox. This will depend on what the owners corporation / body corporate are like. Are they easy to deal with? Are they forward thinking or very conservative? If they are a difficult bunch then you most likely will encounter blocks with any changes you want to make, including installing a lockbox.

10. **Insurance:** You need insurance that specifically covers holiday (Airbnb) rentals. Don't just rely on Airbnb if something goes wrong.

11. **Consider the apartment's strengths and weaknesses:** Strengths include: layout (well-organised and 'Zen' feel), high ceilings, size, view, natural light, access. Weaknesses include: layout (avoid higgledy-piggledy), location in building (next to car park), noise (next to busy street), size (too small) and too dark.

12. **Heating and cooling:** Is there an effective heating/ cooling system?

13. **Capital growth versus bookings potential:** The CBD is often (though not always) the most sought-after place to stay for travellers and guests. However, the CBD is often not the best place for capital growth. You may have to compromise on one to maximise the other.

Checklist 2: Fitting out your apartment – furnishings and style

1. **Interior design:** If you are a dab hand at designing, give it a go yourself, but get some help if you need it. Look around for a decorating service as opposed to a very expensive interior designer (some furniture and homeware stores offer this service). You don't need to spend a fortune on furniture. The main thing is to style your Airbnb so that it is comfortable and welcoming for your guests.

2. **Bed, bedding and manchester:** A good, new, comfortable bed is a must. Pamper your guests with a choice of good pillows, good quality sheets and pillowcases and luxurious towels.

3. **Large screen television:** (put it on the wall if you can) and get Netflix or Stan or another streaming service.

4. **Kitchen:** A coffee machine (or plunger – not instant coffee), a range of teas and some milk will keep guests happy. Provide condiments and good quality pots, pans and utensils.

5. **Prints (or paintings):** Spend money on a few statement pieces like prints. Even one stand-out piece gives the 'wow' factor. Less is more.

6. **Heating and cooling:** Make sure the heater and/or air-conditioner are effective.

7. **Shower:** People like a good hot shower – plenty of hot water and a good shower head are needed.

8. **Clutter:** Keep your Airbnb clutter free.

Checklist 3: Preparing to launch on the Airbnb website

1. **Education:** Find an Airbnb course (online is fine) and do the course before listing. I gained a lot of knowledge and I think a short course is a worthwhile investment.

2. **Photographs:** Using a professional photographer is preferable. Airbnb may offer a free or reduced cost service, or they may recommend photographers. Alternatively, do it yourself if you're confident with a camera, or ask a friend who is great at taking photos to come over and snap away. Take your time and make the effort to get great photos. Use landscape photos in your advertising; they are more appealing.

3. **Blurb for your listing on the Airbnb website:** Your words matter. Look at other blurbs on the Airbnb website as a guide. Don't copy them word for word, but find those you like and use them as inspiration – there's no need to 'reinvent the wheel'.

4. **Highlight your drawcards and accentuate your point of difference.** What does your Airbnb offer that separates you from others?

5. **Pricing:** Start lower than optimal to get guests through the door. Once you are a Superhost then charge appropriately. Guests will pay a fair (higher) price for a fantastic experience.

6. **Cancellation policy:** Strict, moderate or flexible?

7. **Instant book or request to book?** You may get more

bookings with instant book; the flip side is you do not get to 'vet' your guests.

8. **Discounts for longer stays?** Recommended.

9. **Check-in and check-out:** How will it work? Get a process in place to follow. I prefer keyless entry and self check-in. It is essential to develop a process and evaluate how it goes. But remember, make it work for you.

10. **Airbnb website:** It is a powerful tool. Get to know how to use it; it will help you maximise your income.

11. **Cleaner:** Unless you are going to do the cleaning yourself, find a good cleaner as they are worth their weight in gold.

   - Do the cleaning yourself at the start. You will learn how to clean your Airbnb and will be able to do it in an emergency, and you will know what you want from your cleaner.

   - Seek out referrals for good cleaners.

   - Hire a cleaner who already has Airbnb experience, as they will understand the process.

   - Have a back-up cleaner.

   - However good your cleaner is, check your Airbnb before guests arrive (if you can) to ensure the cleaner has done his or her job.

12. **House manual:** Your guests will need to know the wi-fi codes, how to use the TV remote and how to use the coffee machine (if you have one). They will appreciate a comprehensive house manual that covers all these things and lots more.

Checklist 4: Running your Airbnb

1. **No surprises:** Make sure your Airbnb is 'as advertised'. Whether or not you get a five-star review will depend, in part, on whether your guest's expectations are met. If your Airbnb is next to a noisy bar, for example, be up front about it. There is a place in the market for all-comers, but only if you're honest with your guests.

2. **One, two or three?** Work out your minimum night stay. Perhaps start with one night, then move to two and see how you go.

3. **Check your Airbnb before guests arrive:** Don't rely on others. You need to check. Are there fresh towels? Is everything clean? Is the cupboard stocked? Does the heater work? Mistakes will be made, and you need to avoid as many as you can.

4. **Develop systems:** You should develop systems to minimise your workload. For example, have a check-in procedure you follow each time a guest books (information you send out, text messages you send).

5. **Provide that little bit extra (including information about the location):** Guests will appreciate all the little extras and the rave reviews will follow.

6. **Set the tone:** Establish rules and boundaries and apply them in order to keep your sanity. For example, will you allow early check-ins, give discounts, or allow luggage storage. If not, then say so and stick with it.

7. **Keep your cool:** I can guarantee you will get the occasional problematic guest. When you do, keep your cool, make them happy (within reason) and remember the reviews.

8. **Invest in your apartment:** Be prepared to invest in your Airbnb asset and it will repay you ten-fold. If you penny-pinch it will be reflected in your reviews.

9. **Make it work for you:** Make your guests happy, but make sure you're happy too.

10. **Apartment manual:** It will save you time if your apartment manual answers most questions you are likely to be asked.

Checklist 5: Profit and loss

1. **Airbnb.com:** Become very familiar with the website – it has great features, is a fantastic asset and will help you maximise bookings and profits.

2. **Accounting packages:** An accounting package, such as Xero, Quickbooks or MYOB, will help you keep track of your finances. You can use pen and paper if you like, but run your Airbnb like a business because it is.

3. **Income and expenses:** Keep track of all your income and expenses. This will give you a clearer picture of how your business is performing, and keeping an accurate record of expenses will help you maximise your after-tax profits.

4. **Keep your neighbours happy:** If your neighbours complain, it will not only cause you emotional grief and eat into your time, it may also cause you financial grief, so keep them happy.

5. **Owners corporation:** If you own an apartment that is subject to an owners corporation, get onto the committee so that you can monitor your asset and participate in decisions that will affect your business.

6. **Insurance:** Important, especially if your Airbnb burns down. Make sure you have the correct type of insurance (there are several types of landlord insurance), and familiarise yourself with what is covered by the policy.

7. **Price point:** Work out your price point – what you are going to charge guests to stay at your Airbnb. If you've got

a premium product, charge a premium price. Bookings are important, but if you charge peanuts, you may get monkeys.[4]

8. **Be honest:** This applies to your guests and to the taxman. Dishonesty with your guests may lead to bad reviews; dishonesty with the taxman may lead to jail – so best to be honest.

---

[4] I have taken some poetic license here. The proper saying is: if you pay peanuts you'll get monkeys, and it was meant to apply to employer/employee situations, but I think it applies, in modified form, here.

Airbnb Requirements to be a Superhost

- Completed at least ten trips or completed three reservations that total at least one hundred nights
- Maintained a ninety per cent response rate or higher
- Maintained a one per cent percent cancellation rate (one cancellation per one hundred reservations) or lower, with exceptions made for those that fall under the Airbnb Extenuating Circumstance Policy
- Maintained a 4.8 overall rating (this rating looks at the past 365 days of reviews, based on the date the guest left a review, not the date the guest checked out).[5]

[5] Adapted from www.airbnb.com.au/help/article/829/how-do-i-become-a-superhost

Apartment Manual

A very warm welcome and a huge thank you for staying at my little abode. Have a fabulous time in Melbourne and may the apartment feel like a home away from home.

I am contactable via phone or email and I receive all my Airbnb messages on my mobile. If you need help with getting out to the balcony, how to use the TV or appliances, how to get around Melbourne, how to use MYKI or for anything I'm only a phone call or email away and very happy to be of help. My husband Adam is also on hand if I'm not available.

Juls M: 043★ ★★★ ★★★ E: juls@_____
Adam M: 043★ ★★★ ★★★   E: adam.rollnik@_____
Check-In time is 2 pm, Check-Out time is 10 am.

Apartment access codes

Building entry: Code is ★★★★# (the # symbol is on the bottom right of keypad). The green light will come on and then you can enter building.

To open apartment door, place hand on top of the black screen. The numbers will appear and you type in the code ★★★★★★ **(keypad symbol)** which is on the bottom right of the keypad.

Access to balcony

1. Open the shutters, then
2. Pull the two handles firmly towards you and slide to the left, then
3. Lift the latch at the bottom of the French doors and push open.

To close the door, push the latch down and then pull the screen back to the right and it will slot back into place as it has a magnetic backing. The screen door acts as double-glazing to block out the noise. Remember to slide it back into place so as to keep the outside noise to a minimum.

To close the shutter screen doors, you push the right-hand side in first, and then the left-hand shutter door goes on top of the right one.

House rules

- No pets.
- No parties or events.
- We have great neighbours so please be respectful.
- Please keep the noise to a minimum level in the evening.
- Please leave the apartment as you found it.
- When you leave apartment, please turn off the lights and heater/air conditioner.
- The apartment is not suitable for young children because of the balcony.

Smoking

The apartment is non-smoking inside. You can smoke on the balcony and there is an ashtray bucket under the sink in the kitchen for you to use. I would be very grateful if you don't put the butts in the pot plant.

Internet

Connection for the internet is:

Wifi: Telstra ★★★★★★★

Password: ★★★★★★★★★★★★

If for some reason the internet drops out, you just need to reset the modem. It is located in the bedroom, underneath the right-hand side table.

TV

To turn on the TV, press the green button on the top right-hand side of the remote. To change channels you can click on the numbers or use the up and down keys. The volume button is to the left of the program button.

Netflix

To watch Netflix press the 'Home' button, which is the blue button under the circle. Arrow to the right (in the circle) until you come to 'Internet Content'. Arrow up to Netflix and then push the round button in the middle of the remote. It can take a minute or two to upload, so if nothing is happening just give it a minute and then Netflix will appear.

If for some reason the Netflix box does not appear when you come to 'Internet Content', press the black button in the middle of the remote and Netflix will come up. Then just press the middle black button again and it will come on.

A box will appear:

Who's watching – Adam, kids

Click on one of those two options (round button in the middle of remote). You can see what is on Netflix or if you are wanting to search for a show then arrow up and click on Search.

If you want to go back to another program or return to TV then you press the 'Return' button found next to the blue 'Home' button.

If for some reason Netflix doesn't come on or it is saying it's not connected to the internet or if it comes up with 'retry' all you do is press retry. You may have to press 'retry' several times. If it keeps coming up then push 'cancel', wait a few minutes and try again. It will work – it just can be a bit temperamental. Sometimes it can take several attempts and then seems to reset itself or if all else fails you can reset the modem. This should do the trick.

Bose stereo docking system

You can stream your music through your phone and it also works as a charging station for your phone. The system remote is the small one next to the TV remote.

Iron and Ironing board

The iron is in the cupboard above the fridge and the ironing board is next to the fridge.

Supplies and Condiments

Coles and other supply outlets are located at Melbourne Central which is only a 4-minute walk away.

www.melbournecentral.com.au

There are a couple of shopping bags in the drawer under the oven for you to do your shopping as there are no plastic bags at the supermarket.

If you have left your toothbrush or razor at home there are some spares in the cupboard above the fridge.

If you are looking for an umbrella, there is one in the bottom drawer in the kitchen. Also in the drawer is a travel adaptor and an extension lead if you want to use the lamp on the desk.

There are pens on the desk for your use while at the apartment but I would be most grateful if they did not leave the apartment. They are for guest use.

The magazines are for your reading pleasure and also part of the stay.

Ear Plugs

There are some ear plugs/putty in the bathroom cupboard. Construction has gone nuts in Melbourne and from time to time there may be overnight works, or a party happening, or early morning traffic. The ear plugs should help reduce the noise.

Appliances

The dishwasher and washing machine manuals are in the apartment manual in the desk drawer. All other appliance manuals are kept in a folder above the fridge, or drop me a line if you are having difficulty with working out how to use any of the appliances. Google is also a great help.

Coffee Machine

To use the coffee machine, heat the milk first. Fill the frother to the lower line and switch on. Keep your eye on it, as if it's full cream milk it may overflow when heated.

Next, place a pod into the machine, put a cup under the coffee spout, and press the button to indicate small, medium or large coffee. Add the heated milk to the coffee and voila!

The water cylinder is located at the back of the machine and you should ensure it has water in it. Please thoroughly rinse the milk frother after use and leave some water in it. Please only use a soft cloth to clean.

Dishwasher

Push the black button on the right to the 'normal cycle', which is the 4th program selection. The 'on' button is to the left. The cycle should run for about 2 to 2.5 hours.

If hand washing, there is a drying mat under the sink or a dish rack for your use.

Oven

The on/off button for the oven is on the left-hand side of the wall above the power outlet, next to the knife set. It is always on but if for some reason the oven won't work then flick the switch and it should turn it back on. The timer switches for the oven are on the left-hand side of the oven, the heat switches are in the middle of the oven, and the program switches are to the right. The oven section of the manual explains the function of each dial.

Washing Machine/Dryer

The laundry powder goes in the top compartment on the left-hand side of the machine. Pull it out and the powder goes in the first area of the compartment on the left-hand side. As it is a **front loader** machine you only need a quarter of a scoop of laundry powder. Please do not use fabric softener. The cotton cycle or the quick 29 cycle work well. Refer to the manual for alternative cycles. Laundry powder is kept in the cupboard next to the washing machine.

There is a clothes drying horse next to the washing machine if you want to air dry your clothes.

Air conditioner/heater

The remote is on the wall. All you do is press the on button and use the up and down arrows to set the temperature you want.

I would be most grateful if you can please turn the air conditioning/heating off when you are not at home as it can become very expensive if left running when not at the apartment. It is also better for the environment not to have it on while no-one is home. Have it on as long as you like when home. Thank you so much.

Bedside lamps

To turn lamp on and off the switch is on the lamp head.

You can dim the lighting on the lamp. All you need to do is keep your finger on the switch and it will go up and down to the setting you so desire.

MYKI cards

There are two MYKI cards in a pouch in the desk drawer for your use while at the apartment. You can top up the cards at any train station, newsagent or 7/11. Melbourne Central is the closest station and the nearest 7/11 is at ★★★★★★★★★★★★★★★.

Lots of information on how MYKI works is on their website:

http://ptv.vic.gov.au/tickets/myki/

What's on in Melbourne

There are some brochures in the drawer of the desk letting you know what's happening around town.

These websites offer great tips for what's happening across the city:

www.weekendnotes.com/melbourne/
www.airbnb.com.au/things-to-do/melbourne
https://theculturetrip.com/pacific/australia/
articles/21-awesome-free-things-to-do-in-melbourne/
https://theculturetrip.com/pacific/australia/articles/20-
unmissable-attractions-in-melbourne/

The Victoria market is a winner. The Southbank/Casino strip is lots of fun. The Botanical Gardens are lovely. The art gallery or museum may tick your box. If you need help deciding on a particular thing you want to do or a restaurant you may want to go to but aren't sure of, let me know as I may be able to let you know if it's a winner or not.

There is an absolute abundance of fantastic cafes and restaurants at your fingertips including Hardware Société across the way. It is such a popular spot that there is often a line waiting to get in. To the right of the apartment building is Hash which makes the BEST hot chocolate and the food always has flair. CJ Lunchbar is a couple of doors away and is brilliant for a $6 or $7 meal.

La La Land is a fabulous upstairs bar literally a hop, skip and a jump from apartment. It is a great place to unwind and have a drink and is only 2 doors away.

www.lalaland.com.au/melbourne/

To be honest you have such an incredible array of fabulous places to eat in and around Hardware Street. Little Lonsdale Street has some great little cafes and they are sooooo cheap.

Hardware Lane is just down the way and you are spoilt for choice with cuisine.

Getting around Melbourne

There are all modes of transport at your disposal.

Melbourne Central train station is a four to five minute walk away from the apartment.

www.melbournecentral.com.au/

Trams are all very close by and tram travel in the CBD is free! How cool is that.

Journey Planner is a terrific website for all your public transport needs:

www.ptv.vic.gov.au/

journey#jpsearch%5Baction%5D=showPlanner

The Safe City Taxi Ranks are located at various spots in town:

- Queen Street Rank is between Little Collins Street and Bourke Street, in the heart of the city's nightclub precinct. Operating times: Midnight Friday to 5 am Saturday; Midnight Saturday to 5 am Sunday.
- Flinders Street Station, at Swanston Street
- 190 Bourke Street, near Russell Street
- 8 King Street: Operating times:11 pm Friday to 5 am Saturday; 11 pm Saturday to 5 am Sunday.

Shopping

You are in the HUB of Melbourne's shopping district and all on your doorstep. Melbourne Central, Myers, David Jones, The QV Centre to name a few and all within walking distance.

Great website for shopping around town:

www.thatsmelbourne.com.au/

The apartment has a walking score of 100 out of 100 so everything is catered for in very close proximity.

Gym

Anytime Fitness Gym is just around the corner at 280 Queen Street Melbourne, the corner of Queen and Little Lonsdale. They are a 24-hour gym and provide casual work outs.

www.anytimefitness.com.au

Rubbish

The rubbish bin has two compartments. One for rubbish (lined with bag) and the other for recycling. Fresh rubbish bags are under the sink.

The apartment bins are located on the ground floor. If you take the stairs when you come to the ground floor the door is to the left with 'bins and bikes' on it. If you take the lift, when you get out on the ground floor just turn left and you'll go through the stair door and then you'll see the door to the bins. If you let the door go behind you it will shut automatically but if you push it to without closing it, it will not lock, and that way you can just go back up the stairs or back to the lift to go up to the apartment. Don't fret if it does lock as you just walk out the basement door and walk back around to the front of the building and let yourself back in with the codes. The bins are communal so you can put the rubbish in any bin. The green bins are for general rubbish and the yellow bins are for recycling.

Luggage storage

If you are flying in early or flying out late and you need to store your luggage somewhere for the day, these storage companies are great options:

https://bagbnb.com/luggage-storage/melbourne

www.travellersaid.org.au/luggage-storage

www.southerncrossstation.net.au/luggage_services.html

Skybus

Skybus is a fantastic option for getting to and from Melbourne Airport.

Website: www.skybus.com.au/

Fares are $19 one way; $38 return.

Skybus has a free hotel transfer which is fantastic. Click on the free hotel transfer link on their website and it tells you all about the service. You can always get dropped off or picked up at a hotel close to an apartment you are staying at. The closest hotel to Hardware Street is Adina Apartments, 189 Queen Street Melbourne.

Skybus is such a great service and so affordable.

Suggestions and Reviews

There is a book on the desk so please feel free to leave a message about your stay, places you have found that you love, what I can do to improve your stay. All feedback is much appreciated as this helps guide me on how I can make your stay as enjoyable and memorable as possible.

Enjoy,

Juls

Acknowledgements

This book would not have been possible without the help and guidance of some pretty spectacular human beings. I am indebted to each and every one, because without them, *Secrets of a Superhost* would still be an idea.

Bernadette Foley. I am so blessed and grateful to have found my way to you. When I first reached out to you and your client book was full, that did not deter me. I knew you were the one for me. You referred me to the gorgeous Peter Vaughan-Reid to edit and then I came right back to you to help me with the sparkle and magic I wanted for *Secrets of a Superhost* to bring her to life. I am truly indebted to you.

Peter Vaughan-Reid. Peter what a mammoth task you took on in being my editor. The task of sifting through all my 'reviews' to try and choose the best ones for the book was enormous because most of the reviews were bloody outstanding! What a daunting task to be asked to choose the ones that you thought would fit the bill – credit to you for nailing it. Your 'lightning quick' response to my emails was medal worthy. It didn't matter what time of the day I would send an email – morning, noon, night and even weekends, your response was faster than a speeding bullet. Thanks, Peter – excellence is unforgettable and you nailed it.

Adam Rollnik. Boy, what a collaboration! You started me on this crazy ride. You saw in me what I couldn't see within myself. I was the reluctant Airbnb host and the reluctant writer but you wouldn't give up on me. You had an unfailing belief in me. You quietly, and loudly at times, kept persevering with me to undertake these gigantic tasks. Your steely determination, perseverance and never quit attitude were what kept me going through the really tough days where I so wanted to give up. You were the coach I didn't want but the coach I truly needed. I couldn't have done it without you, and for that I am eternally grateful. Thank you for being the organised and structured person I desperately needed. We make a formidable team.

John Fuller, the agent with the 'mostest' – John was instrumental in helping me find my 'dream apartment' and then, at the other end, in helping me find a buyer when it was time to sell the apartment. Our journey had truly come full circle. John sadly passed away in 2021 and the world lost one of the good guys. You really were from a timeless era John and you are missed, my old friend. I have no doubt John you are looking down and are quite chuffed to be part of this story.

And finally Alec and Paris – my children. You are by far the best part of me and are my rock stars. You were the motivation that pushed me to take a chance on myself when the future for our family was uncertain. I love you both to the moon and back and straight into my heart.